REPORT

OF THE

COMMITTEE OF INVESTIGATION

FROM HOUSE OF REPRESENTATIVES, ILLINOIS, TO INQUIRE INTO THE AFFAIRS OF THE

NEW STATE HOUSE.

REPORT OF THE COMMITTEE.

To the Honorable Speaker of the House of Representatives:

The Committee appointed to investigate the work and affairs of the new State House, respectfully report that the Committee have taken a large amount of evidence relating to the subject matter of the resolution under which it was appointed, which is here presented without recommendation other that it be read and printed.

At the request of the State House Commissioners, we present evidence, taken by Commissioners, of one witness, R. P. Morgan, without the knowledge of the Committee, and also some letters which they deem of importance, and we submit as *ex parte* testimony.

All of which is respectfully submitted.

C. A. ROBERTS,
W. M. EGAN,
H. WATSON WEBB.

MINUTES OF THE COMMITTEE.

SPRINGFIELD, *April* 10, 1871.

Committee on Investigation met.

Present, Messrs. Roberts, Egan, McMillan and Fuller—Webb being absent.

It was unanimously agreed by the committee that only the members of the committee, the witnesses on examination, and the State House Commissioners be allowed to be present during the examination of witnesses.

It was further unanimously agreed that the proceedings of the committee be kept strictly secret until ended.

The testimony of W. W. Boyington, of Chicago, architect, was taken down in writing by the clerk.

Committee adjourned until to-morrow, Thursday evening, at half past seven o'clock.

C. C. KOHLSAAT, *Clerk.*

SPRINGFIELD, *April* 11, 1871.

Committee on Investigation met.

Present, Messrs. Roberts, Egan, McMillan and Fuller—Webb being absent.

Mr. Roberts in the chair.

Minutes of the previous meeting were read and approved.

The testimony of Chas. Bolin-Starck, of Springfield, architect, was taken and reduced to writing by the clerk. Cross-examination by Messrs. Bunn and Beveridge, State House Commissioners, was likewise taken down.

Committee adjourned to meet at the new State House at nine o'clock A. M., and in Committee Room at half past seven o'clock, P. M., of Wednesday, April 12, 1871.

C. C. KOHLSAAT, *Clerk.*

SPRINGFIELD, *April* 12, 1871.

Committee on Investigation met, pursuant to adjournment.

Present, Messrs. Roberts (Chairman), Egan, Fuller, Webb, McMillan. Present, also, Messrs. Bunn and Beveridge.

Minutes of the last meeting were read and approved.

The testimony of W. D. Clark, general Assistant Superintendent of work on the new State House, was taken down in full by Volney Hickox and G. W. Hardacre, short-hand reporters.

Committee adjourned, to meet to-morrow at half past seven o'clock P. M.

C. C. KOHLSAAT, *Clerk.*

SPRINGFIELD, *April* 13, 1871.

Committee on Investigation met, pursuant to adjournment.

Present, Messrs. Roberts, Egan, McMillan, Webb and Fuller—Mr. Roberts in the chair.

Present, also, Messrs. Beveridge and Bunn, State House Commissioners.

Henry Rible, of Pekin, Ill., and Syke Watkins, of Carlinville, Ill., bricklayers and masons, were examined by the committee. John M. Van Osdel, architect, of Chicago, was examined on the part of the State House Commissioners; all of the testimony being preserved.

Committee adjourned, to meet at half past seven o'clock to-morrow, Friday, evening.

C. C. KOHLSAAT, *Clerk.*

SPRINGFIELD, *April* 14, 1871.

Committee on Investigation met, pursuant to adjournment.

Present, Messrs. Roberts (Chairman), McMillan, Egan, Fuller and Webb.

Present, also, Messrs. Beveridge and Bunn, State House Commissioners.

The testimony of Mr. Thomas W. Brady, of St. Louis, architect, and Mr. Cornelius Price, of Chicago, bricklayer and mason, was taken in full by Volney Hickox and G. W. Hardacre, phonographic reporters. Committee adjourned.

C. C. KOHLSAAT, *Clerk.*

SPRINGFIELD, *May* 29, 1871.

Committee on Investigation met in Committee Room.

Present, Messrs. Roberts, Egan, Webb and McMillan.

George D. Garnsey, of Chicago, architect, sworn and examined.

Anthony Eitner, of St. Louis, brick mason, and James Appleyard, of Detroit, builder, sworn and examined on the part of the State House Commissioners.

Committee adjourned, subject to call of chairman.

C. C. KOHLSAAT, *Clerk.*

SPRINGFIELD, *May* 31, 1871.

Committee on Investigation met at three o'clock P. M.

Present, Messrs. Roberts, Webb and McMillan.

William Clark, of Springfield, sworn and examined on the part of the State House Commissioners.

Wm. Sands, of Springfield, builder, sworn and examined on behalf of the State House Commissioners.

David Sherman, of Springfield, builder and contractor, sworn and examined on the part of the State House Commissioners.

Alfred H. Piquenard, of Springfield, architect, sworn and examined on the part of the State House Commissioners.

Wm. Shepard, of Jerseyville, Ill., mason, sworn and examined on the part of the State House Commissioners.

C. C. KOHLSAAT, *Clerk.*

SPRINGFIELD, *May* 31, 1871.

Committee on Investigation met in Committee Room.

Present, Messrs. Roberts, Webb and McMillan.

Wm. A. Steele, of Joliet, quarryman, sworn and examined on the part of Committee on Investigation.

George Pipe, of St. Louis, bricklayer and contractor, sworn and examined on the part of the State House Commissioners.

F. Schroeder, of Chicago, brick mason and builder, sworn and examined on the part of the State House Commissioners.

Edwin Walker, of Lemont, quarryman, sworn and examined on the part of the State House Commissioners.

W. D. Richardson, of Springfield, contractor and builder, sworn and examined on the part of the State House Commissioners.

Richard Young, of Springfield, bricklayer and plasterer, sworn and examined on the part of the State House Commissioners.

Committee adjourned.

C. C. KÖHLSAAT, *Clerk*.

EVIDENCE GIVEN BEFORE THE COMMITTEE.

SPRINGFIELD, *April* 10, 1871.

W. W. BOYINGTON examined.—Am an architect, and reside in Chicago. Have lived in Chicago eighteen years, and have been engaged in profession of an architect something over thirty years. Have examined the stone and brick work of the new State House to-day, and have examined the specifications attached to the contract for the building of the new State House: *i. e.*, that contract with Barnard & Gowan. The specifications, I see, require a certain mixture of mortar. (See specifications.) There must be some mistake in the component parts, or the quality of the parts; the mortar, four or five feet from the top of the wall down, is very defective; it seems to be but very little more than dry sand; that is my first observation this morning. I went over again this afternoon, principally on the instigation of the Governor, he being very desirous that I should give it a careful inspection, and found that same fault with the mortar prevailed the whole hight of the wall; it was not so apparent to the eye as it was upon inspection. That's about all there is in reference to brick work. I judge the quality of the brick to be good; didn't measure size of brick; the brick are not so firmly set but that they can be forced into the wall by being struck with another brick, owing to the fact that the mortar is so weak and that they are not sufficiently grouted behind. Judge about one half of the backing of the outside and the internal partitions is built with defective mortar. My impressions are, that the lime must be of a very inferior quality. I think I could make better mortar out of quick lime and loam. I didn't know that any lime was made at Lemont for some years back. I learned, when I first came to Chicago, that they had made lime at Lemont, but abandoned it because it was not good lime; about twenty years ago. (Admitted by Mr. Bunn, Commissioner, that this lime was made at Lemont.) I have not knowledge, of my own observation, as to this lime; the walls seem to be true. The execution in laying the brick work seems to be good; do not know whether they correspond to specifications, as to execution and size, or not; I didn't discover but that the walls were properly bonded. The stone work appears to be very well cut and I find no particular fault with the setting. There must have been an oversight by somebody in allowing the deep rustic joints to be cut on the bottom of the stone, bringing the joint at the bottom of the rustic. I think that about one half of the stone are so laid and cut. The mortar in which the stone is laid is good, I judge. The defect in the rustic joints may be remedied by making a wash or bevel on the lower side of the rustic. I think the stone as good as the Joliet quarries turn out. I should not think it judicious or safe to go on with the building, as contemplated in the plans, without taking down and remedying the defective work in the walls. I judge from the size of the walls so far, that they are to be carried up very heavy. I think the removal of the defective brick work would necessitate the removal of some of the stone work, though the stone work may be strong enough to stand alone should the brick be removed. I examined the brick arches over the cellar; they seem to be very well laid; they seem to be laid in cement. I do not know that iron beams would have been any better than the brick arches; the cost would depend upon the manner of measuring up the brick work. I understand the brick work was measured solid, from the spring of the arch, and if measured solid I think the brick would cost more than the iron. Brick work of that kind is usually measured by actual solid contents. Arch work costs about $2 per thousand more for laying than plain, square walls. I think you would find a lot of brick work pushing out if you were to go on and finish the building upon the walls as they now stand, because of want of bond caused by defective mortar. The weight of the building would have that effect. My impressions are that the setting quality of that mortar has passed its vital action. I don't think it will ever set much more than it is now set; it may become more rigid as it becomes dryer.

Cross-examined by Mr. Bunn.—The walls seem to vary with respect to the quality of mortar used; in some places the wall is

—2

more defective than in others. I think the worst walls, taking the whole hight of them, appear to be the two walls running east and west, each side of the main corridor. It is not an unusual thing for walls to be injured by being exposed to winter weather, for three or four courses from the top. I had walls laid open last winter, exposed, which were not injured. I had others which were, for one or two courses. The mortar was nearly as hard as the brick in the spring. I know C. & P., architects.

Q. Have you any prejudice against any member of the Board of Commissioners, or the architects engaged in constructing the new State House?

A. I have none that would influence my statements at all. These statements can be easily proven.

WM. W. BOYINGTON.

TUESDAY, *April* 11, 1871.

CHARLES BOLIN-STARCK testifies.—My name is Chas. Bolin-Starck. I reside in Springfield. Am an architect and civil engineer. Have lived here one and one-half years. Am forty-five years of age. Have been a civil engineer and architect fifteen years; ever since I came to this country; was one in Europe before I came over; studied and practiced it in Europe before I came to America. I have examined the work on the new State House to-day; never before; I did not make a very close examination, looked over it generally. I examined the brick work; part of the brick walls seem to be sound and good, other parts not. Every part of the brick walls exposed to the weather from above, seemed to be defective for three or four courses; the bricks were loosened by somebody. I judge that several courses of almost all the wall ought to be taken down and reset; the upper courses. I examined the character of the mortar; there were two kinds of mortar—that is, mortar and cement—used in laying the brick. Parts of the mortar was very good, in other places it was not good. I think about one-third is not good; I can't tell exactly; I mean that part of the brick wall above the cellar. The mortar in the bad parts seems to crumble in the hands to dust. Such a wall should not be laid in that kind of mortar. If the mortar was made as it should be made, it wouldn't crumble; the mortar could not have been made of the proper proportions of lime and sand. I have never seen such mortar. I did not examine the materials of which the mortar was made, nor do I know what the mortar was made of. If properly made, it would not have had the appearance it now has. This bad mortar here has a kind of a white color to it. I don't know why this mortar has not the necessary cohesive properties to make it proper mortar to be used in such a wall. The walls are sufficiently thick, but part of them should be taken down before the wall is carried up higher, because several of the upper courses are loose. There are some openings in the inner wall which are some four or five feet from the floor, the walls of which will have to be taken down, because the mortar is bad and the bricks are loose; other portions of the wall, openings in the inner walls, are good—where the good mortar has been used. I don't think that every part of the bad wall will have to be taken down and reset. I can give no estimate of what proportion would have to be so taken down and reset, without a careful examination. I examined the mortar down near the floor; it seems to be generally better; I found no bad mortar near the floor. The bricks were laid in such manner as to have made a good wall, had good mortar been used. The walls are true and plumb, so far as I discovered. If good materials had been used, and the mortar been properly mixed, the weather could not have affected the walls as much as they seem to be affected. The brick appear to be good, so far as I have examined the quality. I don't think the bad mortar used in the State House will improve by age. I did not examine the arches in the cellar; I examined the stone work. There appeared to be some irregularity in the first course of stones above the base, and where the stones were joined. I believe, in every other course, the joint is on the lower side of the groove, so as to admit water into the joint. This will, in time, damage the stone and wash out the mortar. It could be remedied. Cement could be forced into the seam, or a wash or bevel cut in the under stone. In that case the upper side should also be cut to make the appearance uniform. One large sill is cracked. The mortar in which the stone are set seems to be good and the stones well set. I don't think it would materially affect the stone wall to remove the brick work. In case of such removal, a new brick wall could be built and joined to the stone wall and make as good a wall as if the whole had been built together.

Cross-examined by Messrs. Bunn and Beverigde.—I have not made the study of lime, mortar and cements a specialty, any more than was necessary in my business as an architect. I have built or assisted to build in Europe, a very large church. I was not the builder but the architect in Europe. I have also been an architect in New York and Philadelphia. I have superintended the construction of buildings in this country, in Philadelphia—dwelling houses. Quick lime will not harden if hermetically excluded from the atmosphere. It will not harden and set as soon in a two foot wall as in a sixteen inch wall. If the brick are thoroughly wet and each course grouted, it will not set as soon as if the brick had not been wet or the wall grouted. Frost destroys the cohesive qualities of lime mortar, not yet dried, to some extent. If green mortar was to freeze solid, it would wholly lose its cohesiveness. It is possible that the bad brick work in the upper corner may have arisen from climatic influences in some degree, but it would not so destroy the cohesiveness of the mortar as that it would crumble in the hand. Good mortar, frozen solid while green, may lose its cohesive qualities, but will not crumble in the hand, as this. Neither will it crumble as this does, when subjected to both rain and frost while fresh, before it is set or hardened. I do not think this defectiveness extended along the whole length of any one wall. I refer to the top courses. The north wall of the west corridor is the worst, I think. I do not know whether it is the thickest wall or not. Mortar will not harden as quick in a thick wall as in a thin one. There was defective mortar in the whole of the said north wall of the west corridor, so far as I could see. I could discover a difference between the walls laid in quick lime and cement. The wall laid up in cement was good. I do not know the time of the year during which the walls were built. If the material used in mortar which was good was the same as that used in mortar which was bad, the difference would be attributable to climatic influences. If the same quality of lime and sand has been used (in the proper proportions) in the construction of the walls as that used in the concrete stone exhibited to me here, I should pronounce it good. Frost would have no effect on mortar that was thoroughly dry when cold weather came on.

Re-examined. Mortar will not freeze in a thick wall as much as in a thin one. Mortar would not be likely to freeze this winter in the walls under consideration. The winter has been mild. When it was warm enough for the workmen to work, it would not be likely to freeze hard enough to spoil the mortar.

Re-cross-examined. If the walls had been covered, the damaging effects would not have been so great.

C. BOLIN-STARCK.

WEDNESDAY EVENING, *April* 12, 1871.

W. D. CLARK, examined.

Direct—MR. ROBERTS:

Q. State, if you please, what your name is, and where you reside?

A. My name is W. D. Clark, and I reside in Springfield.

Q. How long have you resided here?

A. Came in the winter of '68, I think—three years ago last January.

Q. What is your age?

A. I am fifty years old.

Q. What is your business?

A. Engineer and architect, for the last twenty-three years.

Q. Where have you followed that business?

A. In Lowell, Mass., Nashua, N. H., Davenport, Iowa, and on the DesMoines river.

Q. I will ask you what business you are engaged in now?

A. Assistant superintendent of the construction of the new State House.

Q. Just go on and state how long you have been in that occupation?

A. I came here in January, 1868, as assistant superintendent, under the supervision of Mr. J. C. Cochrane, architect and superintendent of the new State House, and have been thus engaged ever since.

Q. State, if you will, how you have got along, in regard to plans—whether the plans have been regularly furnished, and whether promptly or not?

A. I will state frankly: The first season I came here, the plans were furnished me as soon as it was necessary to commence the excavation of the trenches, and the plan for the foundation was furnished me in May, 1868, and from that plan I have completed the foundation. In the winter of 1869 and 1870 Mr. Piquenard came down as local superintendent, to take charge of the work, and furnished me the plan that I have had to go by—in what has been done the present season.

Q. State whether they were promptly furnished—the plans.

A. So far as the promptness of furnishing the plans was concerned, there has been some delay; but at the same time I don't know that there has been any particular delay, so as to retard the progress of the work.

Q. Whose fault was this; what caused the delay?

A. Well, it may have been from the fact that it wasn't in the power of the superintendent to furnish the plans just at that moment. There was no delay, so far as the progress of the work was concerned.

Q. Who is the superintendent of the work?

A. As I understand it, at the present time, Mr. Piquenard is the superintendent of the work here; Mr. Cochrane is architect and superintendent with Mr. Piquenard, and Mr. Piquenard came here to superintend the construction of the work here.

Q. How much time does Mr. Cochrane spend here?

A. Well, not a great amount of time. He comes down perhaps once a month.

Q. How long does he stay?

A. Perhaps a day or two.

Q. How much time does Mr. Piquenard spend here?

A. All the time. He came a year ago last winter, some time in January, if I recollect right.

Q. Who was superintendent before?

A. Mr. Cochrane was superintendent before he came.

Q. Was he here constantly?

A. No, sir.

Q. What architect was superintending?

A. Mr. Cochrane was superintending, with me as assistant, under the title of clerk of the works.

Q. Are you employed by the architect or the commissioners?

A. I am appointed by the architect and paid by the State, but my appointment was confirmed by the Commissioners.

Q. What salary do you receive?

A. Three thousand dollars.

Q. I will ask you, if you have measured the brick, if you know anything about the number of brick that have been laid in this contract with Barnard & Gowen—the number furnished up to this time?

A. The brick have been measured under my supervision as assistant superintendent.

Q. By whom?

A. By myself and my son, who assisted me.

Q. How much did they amount to?

A. 8,500,000 (eight million five hundred thousand), I think.

Q. Up to what time?

A. To the present time.

Q. You will state, if you please, how that measurement was made—whether the openings are allowed or whether they are deducted?

A. The openings are deducted. It is measured by the actual cubic contents of the walls, including the arches, from the spring of the arch.

Q. How about the openings in the walls—the flues?

A. The flues, the hollow walls and flues, are measured in as solid.

Q. That is done in all cases?

A. Sometimes they have been measured double, but in this case these are measured as specified.

Q. The only openings are the doors and windows, all the balance measured as solid?

A. Yes sir.

Q. Do you know how much stone has been sent by Barnard & Gowan?

A. Not able to tell you. We keep account of the stone—every stone that comes on the ground. If you could see the books you would see we keep a record of every stone that comes upon the ground, on what car it comes, and its cubic contents. We measure it on the cars as it comes in, and as soon as it comes, every single stone. We make the record in the book of the number of the car, the number and letter of the stone, and its dimensions and cubic contents. Then the foreman (Messrs. Barnard & Gowan's foreman) who has charge of the setting of the stone—it is his duty to keep a record of every stone set. We take that, as he sends it, into another book, so we have the number of every single stone set during the progress of the work, and we know where every stone was set, in what wall it was set, and the day which it was set. For instance, the walls are numbered and lettered all around from *a*: the front wall lettered "A;" from there we go around from east to north, and around "A, B, C," clear around. To illustrate, then, the courses being also numbered: "*a*" in "A" wall, is on the east side of the portico, and it contains "No. 1;" it stands in "*a*" wall and in "A" course. Now, we can tell you the day that stone arrived here, and we can tell you the day on which it was set. But supposing "No. 1" stone wasn't here, when we got around to that place, and we had another stone that happened to fill its place, having just the exact dimensions, and say it was "No. 12" stone that filled that place, being already on the ground and "No. 1" stone not yet here. We would put "No. 12" in and record it.

Q. What is your general business in connection with the work?

A. My general duty is the supervision of the work and carrying out the instructions of the architect.

Q. Is it your duty to examine the materials with which the work is being done?

A. Yes sir. It is my duty to see that the work is properly done.

Q. I will ask you, Mr. Clark, if you have examined the mortar and brick with which this brick work is being done?

A. Yes sir.

Q. Just state what is the character of that mortar, how it is made.

A. Shall I state with regard to the brick?

Q. Whether good or not.

A. The brick, in my judgment, are good, and the mortar, so far as I can judge, is good. I hav'nt had experience in the Walker lime used last year. It is possible I may have been deceived, but it is my impression it is good mortar, and so far as I am able to judge, if there is any failure in that mortar it is in the fact that there was more lime used than was necessary. I will state the fact that there is a great deal of diversity among engineers in relation to the mixing up of mortar. The point with me is, that as little lime as you can possibly use, the better, provided it is well beaten. The great secret is to use as little as possible and have it thoroughly beaten. It is just like a glue joint, the closer you can get a glue joint the better. That is my judgment in relation to mortar.

Mr. McMillan:

Let me suggest the parts that entered into the mortar.

Mr. Roberts:

Q. What proportion of lime and sand?

A. We claim to use about from three to five parts sand to one of lime.

Q. Is that about the general proportion?

A. Yes sir.

Q. I will ask you if you superintend and see about the mortar?

A. I am frank to say that I have not been able to attend to all those particulars. I have had all that work to lay out.

Q. Did the architects not lay out the work?

A. I have had it to do.

Q. What do the architects do?

A. They come on and look over the work occasionally, but so far as the general supervision of the work is concerned I have had everything to do myself. I have had every single line to lay out—driven every stake, supervised the—

Q. Then you hav'nt had time to supervise the making of the mortar?

A. Havn't had time to make and furnish to seven or eight walls of brick—couldn't overlook and furnish mortar and attend to the lines.

Q. I will ask you, Mr. Clark, if you know anything about the character of the sand used in making that mortar?

A. Well, so far as the sand is concerned, it is finer than I should choose, but it is perfectly clean. The judgment is, that bank sand is much superior to river sand. River sand is rolled up, and rolling wears the corners off, takes off the sharpness, while bank sand is sharp.

Q. Where did the sand come from?

A. The bank near the Sangamon river, about three or five miles off, I should say.

Q. How long before the mortar is mixed is the lime slacked?

A. We slacked two or three car loads of the lime. The specifications required slacking at least two weeks before using, but this set so it could not be used. We have two thousand dollars ($2,000) worth of lime that cannot be used. It is set and hard. It was claimed that the lime had hydraulic qualities which required it to be used as soon as it was slacked, so that after we had made those experiments, we were required to use the lime immediately after it was slacked.

Q. 'I will ask you if quick lime will act that way?

A. Quick lime won't do it, according to my experience.

Q. State what is your theory in regard to it?

A. My experience in using quick lime is, the longer it is slacked the better. For instance, if a man wants to build a fine house, he slacks his lime and runs it into a bed and covers it up, to be used the following year. That is always considered very much better than to use it immediately after slacking.

Q. State whether this lime is the best quality of lime to be used for the purpose.

A. I am not not prepared to say. My impression is, that it is as good lime as could be used. My impression is, that it has hydraulic qualities in it that make it the first quality of lime.

Q. With regard to the quality of this sand, is it the best quality of sand?

A. I am free to admit it isn't the best quality of sand, because it is finer than I should choose, but it is perfectly clean and clear. It is good as could be got in this part of the country, and I don't doubt its quality—it is perfectly clear from any loam or dirt.

Q. I will ask you if you have examined the mortar within a short time, and if you have, what condition you found it in?

A. My attention has been called to the mortar in the walls. As the walls are thick, every brick was thoroughly saturated before it was laid. There are now places in those open windows where the walls were not thoroughly grouted. As a general rule, so far as I could carry out a rule, I don't allow a single brick to be laid without being grouted out every course. But you are all well aware, that in carrying along a building of that kind I could not watch every course that was laid. So far, however, as I could possibly carry out the rule, I didn't allow a single course laid without being thoroughly grouted. In those openings it was of minor consequence, and of course I didn't pay as much attention there as I might. Now the walls being thoroughly wet—saturated—it takes a long time for them to dry up, and when the frost came, freezing and thawing (we have had a pretty hard winter), the mortar was freezing and thawing all the time, and it had the tendency to kill the mortar two or three courses from the top, and perhaps a little upon the inside.

Q. On those inside walls, up three or four feet from the floor, if the mortar was good and properly laid—laid last October—state if it would be reasonably hardened by this time?

A. No, sir. I have called the attention of several to the mortar that adheres to the wall. If you'll notice that along where the stagings come, where they are using mortar, of course it will splash up against the wall, and you will find chunks as large as your thumb there; it is impossible to pull it off, hard, while the joint right under it you can take your knife and pry it, pick it right out.

Q. Where mortar is made right, five or six months after it has been used, what appearance does it have when you take it out?

A. It is hard; it is almost as hard as brick.

Q. Now in a wall like that, for instance, when you take it out—

A. You couldn't take it out; it would be solid.

Q. When not dry what appearance would it have?

A. Not set at all. Lime mortar doesn't set like cement. Some cement sets quicker than others; some you couldn't use after five minutes.

Q. I will ask you now if it was proper to lay that brick when the weather was such that it didn't set and harden from that time to this, as far up, for instance, as three or four feet from the floor?

A. Did you ask me if it was proper? I will state that the walls which show the most defect were laid in August and September, while the walls that appear the most perfect, were laid during the cold weather. The point is here, it is a rule after the frost comes, after we have hard frost, we never wet brick. I think thorough investigation will show that the walls that were laid during cold weather—after the cold weather came, and were not wet—do not show the effect of the weather so much as those laid during August and September. [To the Reporter : Don't use the word defect; I mean affected by the weather.]

Q. It takes a thick wall longer to dry than a thin one ?

A. Of course, especially when it is thoroughly saturated. It will take a long time for the whole to dry out, and the mortar to become thoroughly hard, when the brick are all wet.

Q. Where the wall is no more than eight inches thick, and laid last October, finding some defect there, if you got out dry sand, what would you attribute that to ?

A. If you find it all dry sand, I should conclude at once that there was no mortar; that the mortar was not properly made. But so far I have not seen any thing of that. My attention hasn't been called ——

Q. If you were to find five or six feet from the floor, the same state of affairs, where the wall is thick, what would you attribute it to—only dry sand ?

A. If it was dry sand, I should attribute it to its not being thoroughly mixed.

Q. If it was damp sand ?

A. If it was damp, and worked out, I should want to examine whether it was the effect of the frost, or from the mortar not being properly mixed—the mortar not being good quality.

Q. You say the only architect here is Mr. Piquenard. What does he do ?

A. His business is to attend to furnishing the plans, and to have a general supervision. I am working under his direction. He is living on the ground there, and it is his duty to look after the work.

Q. State whether he does that regularly.

A. He is absent some times—occasionally comes around in the morning. I am free to confess he has not been as prompt as I should prefer he should have been.

Q. State whether there has been any delay.

A. Can't say that there was any delay, because I have gone right on.

Q. Who prepares the estimates ?

A. I figure up the estimates and hand them to Mr. Beveridge, clerk of the board.

Q. How often do you make those estimates ?

A. Once a month.

Q. Do you make them upon an exact measurement?

A. As near as we could get it; we made out the stone from our book, because we had the record there of every day's work. But the measurement of the walls, and all that sort of thing, we come at as near as we can.

Q. Could you tell by your measurement how many brick there are?

A. We have that measured out upon our books.

Q. Got your book with you?

A. I haven't.

Q. I think you said the amount of eight million five hundred thousand (8,500,000)?

A. I think in the neighborhood of that, about.

Q. State whether the walls ——

A. I may be mistaken; it may be seven millions (7,500,000).

Mr. Beveridge:

Seven and one half; I gave you the figures.

Mr. Roberts:

Q. State whether the brick work for the basement is done.

A. Yes, sir; all, except filling in the ends of the beams.

Q. State whether you know those basement walls have been made true and correct.

A. As far as our knowledge goes.

Q. State whether, in your judgment, the work is being done according to the contract and plans.

A. So far as the work is concerned, I have full confidence in it. There may be some failures in the brick or masonry; but I took exact care to see that everything was done thoroughly.

Q. I will ask you if you have been able to give the absolute attention to all of it that it demanded.

A. I think I haven't been able to give it all the attention that every part of it demanded.

Q. That is, there wasn't sufficient force—whose fault?

A. I don't know that I can ascribe any fault to any individual particularly. Mr. Piquenard's duty was a general supervision of the work, and to see that everything was carried out according to plans and specifications. He lived there, and if there was any neglect, it wasn't intentional on the part of any one particularly.

Q. How much time does Mr. Piquenard spend about the building?

A. Not a very large portion ; sometimes away for a week or two, coming on the ground perhaps once a day and spending 15 or 20 minutes. I don't think he spends more than 10 or 15 minutes.

Q. Giving that attention to the work as an architect, and as general superintendent, I understand ?

A. I understand that he is general superintendent—local superintendent here—being in partnersbip with Mr. Cochrane.

Q. State whether in that time he can give the attention to the work that a general superintendent ought to.

A. I am free to admit that I should have preferred more of his time if I could have obtained it.

Mr. Fuller.

Q. What portion ought he to devote? Should he be there all the time ? What is his duty ? Is it his duty to be there ?

A. As I understand—Mr. Bunn and Mr. Beveridge can explain —as I understand he is local superintendent out here—has charge of the work, and I am under his direction. I obey his instruction, as superintendent of the work here, in conjunction with the commissioners, of course. It is his duty to have the general supervision of the work, and I claim that it is his duty to come to the works as often as possible, and give me instructions, and if I am not attending to the work—if the work is not being constructed as it should be, it is his duty to tell me and have it corrected.

Mr. Roberts :

Q. Does he ever do that ?

A. Yes, sir.

Q. What errors have been corrected that he has found out ?

A. In several instances he has examined the walls, found defects and called my attention to have it corrected.

Mr. Egan :

Q. I wanted to ask Mr. Clark why those seams were grouted after the walls were laid ?

A. I never grouted the walls.

Q. Not the walls ; the seams. Why is the materials for grout ing spread upon the seams of the walls, after the walls are laid, on top of the mortar ?

A. There has nothing of that kind been done.

Q. There hasn't ?

A. Not to my knowledge.

Q. Then I am in great error.

A. Perhaps you don't understand.

Q. Well, sir, I understand; I know what grouting is: It is filling the brick up; filling up every interstice. Why is a portion of that grouting material placed in the seams of the brick? That is what I want to know.

A. The point is here. Perhaps you know how the brick is laid: They spread the mortar, and they will cut it this way, then strike the trowel, and then lay the next brick to it. When they turn the grouting in, there is a hollow left here to be filled. The cross-joint may not be filled at the outer edge. When they turn that grouting in, it breaks through and runs down.

Q. That's not what I am speaking of. I mean the grouting placed upon the horizontal seams after the wall is laid; because you can go there and take the grouting off.

A. That has not been done. Now, there was a gentleman there the other day, who made this assertion: He would go around on those walls and pick the outside course, and pronounce it good mortar. He claimed to be a builder, as I understand it. Now he asserted——

Mr. McMillan:

We'll bring that out from Mr. Bunn.

Mr. Webb:

Q. I want to ask you, Mr. Clark, whether that pointing is done with the same mortar?

A. There has been no pointing done there.

Q. Is that pointing spoken of by Mr. Eagan—is that the same mortar as that which is proved not to be dry?

A. Precisely the same as the brick is laid in, and if you will reflect a moment you will see that it will cost more to clear out those joints—as the brick is only eight inches long, and two inches thick—to go to work and scrape out all those joints.

Q. Out of the same wall, then, when you find mortar that is dry, it seems to be good mortar, but the moment you take that off, it seems to be not so good?

A. The mortar behind that is not set at all.

Mr. Egan:

I only ask that question to support my own position. I claimed that it wasn't pointed. I was contradicted by Mr. Bunn.

Mr. Bunn:

No, sir.

Mr. Egan:

Some gentleman said it wasn't pointed, but that it was the grouting placed upon those seams.

A. I couldn't understand what you were driving at—pointing and grouting.

Mr. Egan:

But that the grouting material had been placed upon those seams: I didn't think that it could be possible.

A. Any man of common sense would say that that thing could not be done.

Mr. Egan:

I didn't know but my common sense was overcome. The clerk stood by and heard me say it was strange.

A. The whole corroborates the assertion that the mortar must be pretty good, because the mortar adheres to the brick, and you will find chuncks of mortar adhering to the bricks, as large as my thumb—can't pull it off, can't cut it off—and it is of the same material exactly.

Mr. Webb:

Q. The mortar that appears now on the top of the wall: is that the same, now, that is used all through the wall?

A. Yes, sir.

Mr. McMillan:

I will get you to state what kind of mortar was used in setting the stone?

A. The same that was used in setting the brick.

Q. Mortar made of the same parts?

A. Yes, sir; designed to be the same.

Q. State, if you will, whether you gave attention to the setting of the stone?

A. Well, I gave attention to getting the lines of the stone, and so far as I could, I attended to the setting of the stone. We had a foreman as stone setter, in whom we all put a great deal of confidence, and I didn't give it that attention that I would, perhaps, under other circumstances. Mr. Napier, the foreman, is a man of very wide reputation. He had charge of the stone.

Q. State whether they were cut in a workman-like manner.

A. I judge that they were.

Q. Please explain why it is that in one or two places on the west side of the building, just underneath the cornice, there appear some strips of wood.

A. The cornice is in two pieces, you will notice. There is the bottom in one, and the top in the other. The bottom mould was cut out of a stone too narrow; coming to set them in green mortar, they were liable to tip outside.

Q. By reason of the outward projection? Please explain, so that the reporter can take it down.

A. Yes, sir; by reason of the outer projection the stone lying upon green mortar, was liable to tip out, and required wedges in some instances to keep the stone from tipping over, until the mortar should become set, and until the stone above, which was wider, was set in and held in its place.

Q. Will you now state why the first stone you spoke of was cut from a narrow piece?

A. It wasn't deemed necessary to have it so wide, and besides having a narrow stone on the bottom, and a wide one on top, formed a binding and tied it in the brick walls.

Q. Will you state whether or not the placing of a wooden strip——

A. Not a wooden strip—it is a wedge.

Q. ——Injures the wall in any way?

A. Not in my judgment at all. Because when the mortar becomes set it makes a perfect bed.

Q. State whether or not it was necessary to protect the under stone?

A. It was necessary in order to confine the stone to its place so that it should not tip over—the mortar being green—to wedge it on the outer edge, else it would tip down—crush the mortar down and break out. With the wedge, the other stone would make a perfect bed.

Q. Well, I'll get you to state, whether or not the use of those wooden wedges injures the joint in any respect

A. No sir. The presence of the wooden wedges doesn't make a very fine appearance. They should have been cut out close to the wall and then they would not have been discovered. They are no detriment at all.

Q. How thick were the wedges?

A. The wedges were just the thickness of the joints. I am not able to state exactly. I don't make any statements unless I know. Perhaps a quarter of an inch.

Q. State whether or not, in the setting of the first course of stone, wooden wedges were used around the entire building.

A. Not generally. Sometimes there was bed enough so that it did not tip. Sometimes one stone was narrower than another, but generally wooden wedges were only used when it was absolutely necessary to prevent tipping.

Mr. Webb:

Q. I would ask, if the seams where those wedges appear are not to be pointed up?

A. They are all to be cut out.

Q. Are they not all to be pointed?

A. Yes, sir.

Q. Is it usual to leave them that way?

A. Yes sir; and then at last make a trip, and clean them all out at once. That is the specification, that the joints are to be cleaned out—while the stone was being set, the joints were to be cleaned.

[Mr. Roberts here repeated his question, and received the same answer again in reference to the measurement of openings and flues in the walls.]

Q. I wanted to ask you, Mr. Clark, about these arches in the cellar, if you know anything about how they were measured?

A. They were measured solid from the spring of the arch.

Q. State whether that is the usual way of measuring that kind of work?

A. So far as my experience goes, that is the usual way, and as I understand the specifications, all the openings are to be taken out, excepting from the spring of the arch, which was to be measured solid.

Q. What difference does it make in the number of brick, measuring those arches solid?

A. Could not tell.

Q. Could you arrive at any thing like an approximate number?

A. Could'nt guess.

Mr. Webb:

Q. In reference to that one question: Is that custom of measurement usual, owing to the fact that more work is required in making the arch?

A. Yes, sir, that's the reason. So far as my experience is concerned, it is the universal custom to measure solid from the spring of the arch. In some places they measure in all the openings. The specifications here require all the openings to be taken out.

One point, perhaps, isn't generally understood. [You may take this down or not.] The general rule is, in all brick work, that the carpenters shall furnish the centers. The contractor here was to furnish all the centers—furnish them at his own expense—while the rule, the universal rule, is, that the carpenter should furnish them.

Mr. Roberts:

Q. What centers?

A. The centers on which the arches are turned.

Mr. Bunn:

You may state the character of some of the centers.

Mr. Roberts:

I would suggest to the Commissioners to conduct the cross examination through some one or any of the committee. In that way we can get along faster.

Cross-examined by Mr. Webb, on behalf of the Commissioners.—State whether or not there was a good deal of difficulty in setting those centers.

A. Yes, sir; and especially in the centre—the dome center; the other centers required a good deal of attention and a good deal of labor.

Q. By whom was that expense incurred?

A. By the contractors.

Q. That is not the usual custom, is it?

A. No, sir; it is not the rule, unless expressly stipulated.

Q. State what position you occupy there upon the building.

A. My position is assistant superintendent, under the direction of the architects and commissioners.

Q. Did you have the general supervision of the work?

A. I have the general supervision, under the direction of the architects.

Q. The architect, you say, is not there very frequently?

A. He is not there always.

Q. He gives you directions, but the immediate general supervision of the work is in your hands, is it not?

A. The general supervision is in my hands—carrying out the designs and instructions of the architects.

Q. State if it is not the duty of the architect to furnish you the plans, and then your duty to see that the plans are worked up to?

A. It is the duty of the architect not only to furnish the plans, but to have the general suporvision of the work; he is the architect and the superintendent, I am under his instructions.

Q. Who employs you?

A. I am paid by the State; I received my appointment from the architect.

Q. Subject to the approval of the commissioners?

A. Of course.

Q. Then, if appointed by the architect, with the approval of the commissioners, are you not carrying out the duties of the architect, except furnishing the plans?

A. Yes, sir; so far as carrying out his instructions is concerned.

Q. State whether the architect is not under the control and supervision of the commissioners.

A. I understand he is.

Q. What would be the appearance of the mortar dug out from those joints, if it was not thoroughly dry?

A. It would have the same appearance as when laid in the wall.

Q. Would it adhere together or would it have a loose and sandy appearance?

A. It would have a loose and sandy appearance, of course, if it was not set.

Q. State if that would be any evidence that it was poor mortar, if the life of the mortar was killed.

A. No, sir, it would not. If the life of the mortar had been killed or frozen, it would be no evidence that it was poor mortar.

Q. State whether mortar having that appearance is any evidence that its qualities had become killed, or whether it had not become set.

A. It would become set when the walls became thoroughly dried out; it would be no evidence that its qualities were killed;

but possibly after mortar has been frozen several times, it might not become set at all.

Q. What is your opinion of the general character of the brick work here?

A. My opinion has been, that the work was well done—as good as any in the country. That is not only my opinion, but the opinion of competent architects.

Q. Is the mortar that appears between those bricks the same as that upon the outside?

A. It is precisely the same.

Q. State whether the same mortar was used in making the concrete?

A. I would not state positively. I am laboring under the impression that the concrete was laid with half lime and half cement. Mr. Piquenard had a man that did that work, and attended to that part of the work. I may be deceived upon that point, but I am laboring under the impression that it was half cement and half lime.

Q. State whether, from your observation and supervision of the brick work, in your opinion, it would be necessary to take down any part of that work?

A. I should judge it might be necessary to take down a few courses where the weather affected it materially.

Q. How many courses?

A. Perhaps some two or three courses in some places, others not so much. But so far as the vork upon the walls is concerned, I would risk my life upon it to-day.

Q. You would risk your reputation as a builder upon that work?

A. Yes sir, I most assuredly would.

Q. State whether your instructions were not from both the architects and the commissioners to see that the work was properly done?

A. Yes, sir. I had no other instructions, at all.

Q. You had those instructions?

A. Yes, sir. I had such instructions, and I feel that I have done so.

Q. What effect has the weather, such as we have had during the last winter, had upon the mortar?

A. The winter has been a very changeable one, from extremely cold to quite warm weather, continually freezing and thawing, which was very much worse than continued cold weather, and has had a tendency to effect the mortar and make it crumble from the joints.

Q. What experience have you had in building?

A. I have had experience in building for the last twenty years, more or less.

Q. How much of that time?

A. A good portion of the time.

Q. State if you have ever known walls, unfinished as those are, standing out through such weather as we have had during the last winter, that appeared better than those walls?

A. I am free to admit, in my experience with walls, taken in the condition of these walls, they will show the effects of the weather; they would be more or less affected.

Q. If these walls are defective, or if the mortar is defective, whose fault is it?

A. If the mortar is defective, I don't know that we could charge it to any particular fault, or to any particular individual, except to the persons mixing the mortar. So far as I was able to do so, I attended to it strictly. I was very particular to have the mortar thoroughly mixed, and everything done in the best possible manner.

Q. State what was the action of the Commissioners with regard to seeing that the lime, sand, brick, and all the materials used, was the proper materials to be used?

A. So far as my knowledge extends, they attended to that matter. So far as I knew, the mortar, sand, brick and everything was approved by the Commissioners.

Q. They were watching the matter?

A. Yes, sir.' Mr. Beveridge, one of the Commissioners, gave it his attention every day. There was hardly a day in the week but that he was there.

Q. State whether you ever saw any conduct on the part of any of the Commissioners to favor the contractors, so far as the materials or the working of the men was concerned?

A. No, sir, I never did.

Direct Examination resumed, by the Chairman, Mr. ROBERTS:

Q. What are the component parts of the mortar with which these brick are laid?

A. I stated from three to five parts of sand to one part of lime. Engineers differ very widely in the component parts of which mortar should be made. Some will go so far as to use seven parts of sand to one part of lime. The secret of making good mortar is to have put into it just lime enough to adhere the particles, and then have it well beaten up.

Q. Why did it vary from three to five parts of sand?

A. When in the mixing we had cement it took more sand.

Q. Did you put cement in it?

A. We did in the basement.

Q. Did you in the brick work above?

A. When we commenced using the Lemont lime we used cement, but it was conceded that it had hydraulic qualities and did not require cement, and then we did not use so much sand.

Q. You did not use the cement all through?

A. No, sir. I suppose you are aware in doing a job of that kind, we cannot measure the exact quantity of sand. We put in one shovel full of lime and from three to five of sand. But the particular thing in having mortar made well and rich, is to have it mixed well. The brick mason can always tell whether he has good lime by the working of the trowel. Sometimes it may take a little more sand and sometimes a little less. There is no economy in using poor mortar, because it works badly and requires more trouble to lay it. They want the mortar so it will work smooth and nice.

W. D. CLARK.

THURSDAY EVENING, *April* 13, 1871.

HENRY RIBLETT examined:

Direct—By Mr. ROBERTS:

Q. You may state your name, age and place of residence?

A. My name is Henry Riblett. I live at Pekin, Tazewell county, and have lived there since November 18, 1836, and have no other home.

Q. State your profession?

A. Since 11th of April, 1837, until the last six years, I have been a brick layer.

Q. Have you examined the brick work in this State House?

A. I have, to-day.

Q. State what sort of an examination you made, and the result?

A. Well, I noticed first coming there, I noticed first the sand piles; there are apparently two qualities of sand there. Don't consider either of them the first quality for building. That's my judgment about it. I saw none of the lime; I don't know what that is. But when I came up I looked at the work on the foundation story of the building, the brick work, what I got at, and when I got above I was convinced that if I had the control of the job, I would not, for my reputation, have had the job so much damaged for want of covering over during the winter. Those walls I am satisfied have been damaged by exposure during the winter. In portions of it the mortar is not cemented to the work, and I think for two reasons. In the first place, it froze when it was green. My theory is, that mortar once badly frozen and thawed out will never make a cement; that is just my opinion about it.

Q. State what the condition of that mortar is in the basement story, the upper story, as it is now?

A. The mortar, where it wasted down from the work—and perhaps you will understand that term—was hard, but the mortar in the walls is not hard, nor according to my judgment, gentlemen, do I believe it ever will become hard.

Q. State whether you think those brick walls good or not?

A. Well, to appearance, the work is better than the attention it received, excepting the damage it received from frost.

Q. State whether it is suitable (the foundation walls) to put a large building upon, without being taken down, either wholly or partially?

A. I think if I had anything to do with it I would take part of those brick walls down, if my reputation were at stake.

By Mr. Egan:

Q. Why would you take them down?

A. Because I don't consider them as good as they should be. They are damaged, as I said before, by exposure. I won't say that I would take all down, because there are some walls there, perfect, but there are some walls there that ought to come down, according to my judgment.

Q. Why would you be induced to take them down—on account of danger or anything of that kind?

A. Because it is not the kind of work I should like to turn out. My reputation—

Q. Do you consider it dangerous or unsafe to erect a building upon that kind of wall? State whether you consider it unsafe or dangerous?

A. The walls may possibly stand. I could only give them a casual examination. I could tell better if I had pulled down part of it. But from the appearance of the walls—some of them—I would rather take them down.

Cross-examination by Mr. Webb :

Q. Do you mean to say that the work wasn't well done?

A. I did'nt say so. To appearance, the work was well done, but damaged by exposure.

Q. You don't mean to say that the work was well done and that the material was bad? the difficulty was in exposure to the weather.

A. So far as I can see, the difficulty is there.

Q. When you say you wouldn't risk your reputation, you don't mean that the work wasn't well done at the time, but from its appearance at this time.

A. The appearance don't indicate, because it is damaged. It is imperfect; it is not in a perfect state now.

Q. I understand owing to the weather?

A. So far as I could see, had a damp appearance. I think that is the appearance, because the mortar is injured in some of the walls, 'way down, clear below the top. It indicates it by scaling off. An outside wall that scales off shows that it has had exposure to the weather, and it will continue to wash out after the scaling begins.

Q. Wouldn't any brick wall, uncovered and exposed to the weather through the winter—wouldn't some of the layers on top have to be removed?

A. Always almost, unless you cover it carefully.

By Mr. Fuller :

Q. Could you form any opinion as to the quality of the mortar when it was layed, whether good or not?

A. Couldn't, very well; the waste appeared to be good and hard; by that you understand the drippings from the work seasoned.

By Mr. WEBB:

Q. These walls in the interior—these brick walls—would they in the condition they now are, to be plastered onto, would they be seriously injured?

A. I don't know whether they would or not; don't know how much heft they have to bear.

By Mr. McMILLAN:

Q. I will get you to sta te, sir, if you please, what character of lime was used?

A. I can't tell you, didn't see any lime.

Q. Get you to state, whether you examined the mortar?

A. The waste and mortar seasoned before it was frosted, seemed to be good, but the mortar in the walls way down, isn't so good. And I think that's my own theory about frosted and thawed brick work. It is this, in consequence of the freesing and thawing, all the qualities of the cement are destroyed. A chemical change takes place which makes it bad cement.

Q. Please tell, what time did you stand there, examining the condition of the walls?

A. A couple of hours, I should think.

Q. Please state whether you examined the walls generally, in the building, with respect to their qualities and condition?

A. I was around through the the greatest part in the second story, and on the ground work, the foundation, as you term it. The foundation is a good wall, as I said before.

Q. Did you find the work done in a workman-like manner?

A. As far as I could see, yes sir; now, I don't know what the specifications were, but the supports of the walls there didn't indicate being slushed, or grouted, as it is termed.

Q. You speak of portions of the wall not having been grouted?

A. Yes, those portions in the opening. Those openings were protected by arches to support the pressure of the top building. However this didn't amount to much; there is a good permanent arch over the top, and there is nothing there to crush that part.

Q. State whether grouting the walls would have strengthened the building any?

A. Don't know that it would; don't think it important.

Mr. Fuller.

Q. State if you have formed any estimate of the amount or proportion that would have to be taken down?

A. I didn't.

Q. You didn't examine the wall as to the grouting?

A. Only when they were broken. I didn't break the wall.

Q. Did you see any other places?

A. There are other places where the mortar indicated being injured by the frost.

Q. As to the grouting?

A. No, sir. Only where there was slushed over on the outside; that might be done by rain storms, catching the works when the the mortar was green. The mortar would wash down then, as much as slushing, almost.

HENRY RIBLETT

—

Sykes Watkins examined:

Direct.—Mr. McMillen:

Q. State your name and residence?

A. My name is Watkins. I live in Carlinville.

Q. Your age and occupation?

A. I am 39 years of age, and a bricklayer.

Q. How long have you pursued that?

A. Nineteen or twenty years.

Q. State whether you are acquainted with the new Capital building.

A. I was examining it to-day.

Q. What is your idea of the brick work done there?

A. Well, I have examined the work pretty thoroughly to-day, and I think the quality of the work is good.

Q. State what character of examination you made.

A. I have examined the walls at the surface. I also have torn down a portion, and examined to satisfy myself.

Q. Well, state what condition you found the mortar, &c.

A. The brick are laid in what I regard the very best manner. The mortar is somewhat injured—that is, on the top of the walls, by the action of the weather. There has been a freezing of the joints, so that a portion of the mortar has fallen out.

Q. State whether you found the mortar dry.

A. I found the mortar moist, except on the outside of some of the walls where it was beginning to assume a hardening condition.

Q. Had this mortar ever been dry in the interior of the wall?

A. No, sir. Don't think it ever was.

Q. State whether the moist mortar on the interior of the wall had ever been frozen.

A. Don't think it had.

Q. Had the mortar any adhesive power? State whether age would increase that power.

A. Think it will improve it certainly.

Q. Walls no longer erected than those, are they usually found in a better condition?

A. Well, I think that walls no longer erected than those—in other words, I think those walls are in as good condition as could be expected, being exposed as they were to rain and snow—snow and ice lying on top of them during the winter, and running down the surface, freezing and thawing.

Q. State whether or not you didn't find the mortar on the exterior and also in the joints the same.

A. Yes, sir. From half to three-quarters of an inch of the joints had fallen out owing to the frost.

Q. Is that so usually?

A. Yes, sir. That is usual; any mortar will fall out when exposed to the weather—freezing and thawing.

Q. State whether or not that which scales off is not composed of a different material than that used in the wall.

A. I think the mortar on the outside surface is the same as that throughout the entire wall. There are some walls there built of cement mortar, and others of lime and sand mortar.

Q. You think there are not two kinds of mortar in the same wall?

A. I didn't see any indications of that at all.

Q. State whether you regard the brick work as first class work?

A. I do, sir.

Q. What time did you spend in making the examination?

A. An hour in the forenoon, and an hour and a half—probably two—hours, since dinner.

Q. Did you examine the walls about the building, generally?

A. I didn't tear down part of every wall, but I tore down a part of one of the thickest walls, and took three courses off of the top.

Q. What was the relative condition of those walls?

A. They were in good condition. A portion of one of the walls I tore down, in trying to separate the mortar from one of the bricks, the brick split in the center, as I struck it in the side with a hammer.

Q. Which did you find in the best condition, the thin or the thick walls?

A. I think the thick walls were in the best condition.

Q. What is your explanation?

A. The thin walls are more exposed on the outside to freezing. That's the way I account for it.

Q. State whether you found the walls true or not.

A. Yes, sir; all the walls I examined were true.

Q. Did you examine the sand from which the mortar was made?

A. Yes, sir.

Q. What kind of sand did you find it to be?

A. What is termed bank sand.

Q. State whether of good quality?

A. Yes, sir; good quality.

Q. Do you know the lime made at Lemont?

A. Not much acquainted with it; never worked it.

Q. Did you examine any lime about that building?

A. I examined some lime there, reported to be Lemont lime, slacked last fall.

Q. What quality?

A. Apparently of good quality; but of that I couldn't judge so well as I could after it was made into mortar.

Cross-examination by Mr. Roberts, on behalf of the Committee.

Q. Lime that has been slacked for some time, can you not tell the quality of it?

A. Yes, sir; a man can judge, but in order for me to give an opinion of the quality of lime I should rather see it worked, or work it. I would not feel warranted in giving an opinion of lime unless I had used some of it, or unless I saw some of it before it was slacked.

Q. What was the condition of this lime that was slacked there? Was it powdered and soft?

A. Some of it was; having been laid in an exposed condition all winter.

Q. Was it soft and powdered?

A. Some of it was; some of it seemed hard.

Q. If good lime is allowed to lay out in that exposed condition through the winter will it not become powdered like dirt, or will it get into cakes and harden?

A. I think it will become powdered to a certain extent. In laying exposed to the weather a portion it will become powdered, and other portions will remain in cakes. It will be in strata.

Q. Suppose walls were laid last July and August, nine inches thick, would such walls become dry by this time.

A. No, sir, I think not.

Q. How long does it take such walls to dry.

A. It will not dry short of a year.

Q. Will a thin wall dry out quicker than a thick wall.

A. Yes, sir.

Q. Would not those nine-inch walls dry out if they were laid from July to October last, so as not to freeze during the winter—such a winter as last winter?

A. I think not; especially with continued rain and snow, freezing and thawing.

Q. Suppose you could dig three or four inches into those walls, put up in October last, and bring out dry and powdered material like sand, would you consider the mortar good? Say three or four feet from the bottom of the walls?

A. I would, sir.

Q. Would that have cement in it if it came out dry?

A. Yes, sir; I think you can powder any sort of mortar, unless it be cement, not laid longer than that time. You can find mortar that will pulverize. I know from experience in building walls, that it takes from twelve to eighteen months and two years, according to the thickness of the walls, for it to become thoroughly dry, or to undergo the hardening or setting process.

Q. Do you know anything about the quality of this bank sand, except from your examination of it to-day?

A. I have worked this sand some little.

Q. Do you consider it first class sand.

A. Well, I have seen better bank sand than that.

Q. Do you know whether this Lemont lime is as good as the Alton, or lime in other parts of the country?

A. I do not know.

By Mr. Fuller:

Q. Do you consider those walls materially injured by the frost?

A. I do not; except there may be a portion of two walls there that is materially injured. The top of all of them is, perhaps, injured to a certain extent. I found perhaps three walls that are injured down near the bottom—walls that run east and west, right under the arch. They have been tampered with a good deal. The mortar seems to have been washed out more than in any other portion of the walls. Those walls are injured, but I do not think they are materially injured in any other place.

Q. Are there not walls there that should be taken down?

A. No, sir, I think not; except those I have spoken of, and, perhaps about three courses off the tops of the walls. That would be the extent of all that it would be necessary to rebuild.

Q. You think the mortar is good, and all that is necessary to make it adhesive to the brick is time to dry?

A. Yes, sir.

By Mr. McMillan:

Q. Do you think, sir, it would be safe to erect walls to the hight of forty or fifty feet upon those walls as they now stand?

A. I do, sir. I don't think the walls are materially injured. Those places I spoke of are in such a position that there will be no weight upon them. The arches take it off.

SYKES WATKINS.

—

John M. Van Osdel, examined by Mr. McMillan, on behalf of the Commissioners, in answer to a summons by telegraph from C. A. Roberts, Chairman of Committee on Investigation of State House:

Q. State your name, age, residence and occupation.

A. My name is John M. Van Osdel; my age is fifty-nine years; my residence is Chicago; my occupation is an architect.

Q. State what experience you have had as an architect, and what experience as a builder?

A. I have been engaged in building for forty years, and as an architect since 1845—twenty-five years.

Q. State whether or not you have examined the work upon the new capitol building at this place, and if you state that you have, give as concisely as you can the result of that examination.

A. I have examined the work to-day. I examined the mason work of the new State House and find the work well done. The brick are of good quality. The mortar used in the brick-work is, in some places, of quick lime and in other places of water lime. I have no hesitation in saying that the mortar of both kinds is of good quality, and will, in proper time, form a hard cement, which it has already done when the circumstances have been favorable. A small proportion of the walls have been injured by exposure to storms before the mortar had sufficient time to set, and the fact that the bricks were saturated with water before they were laid, and the liquid mortar or grouting being poured upon every course after it was laid, completely saturated the walls with water, and on this account the mortar set very slow, and, therefore, gave opportunity for the storms to affect the joints. The mortar cannot harden until it dries, and many of the walls, on account of their great thickness are yet very damp, consequently the mortar in such walls, although it has set, is still damp and comparatively soft, but will harden as the wall dries and not before. A few courses of the tops of some of the walls will require to be removed. In other places the frost has scaled off the mortar joint, which may be pointed up on account of appearance but does no harm otherwise.

The cut-stone work is well done and has been handled with great care. The joint in the rustic at top or bottom is immaterial. I would prefer it at the bottom, as the joint would be hid from view. The walls interior and exterior have been kept in line with great care, and I have examined the work with much pleasure and satisfaction. The long time required to dry the walls will be of benefit to them, as the cement will be firmer on that account.

Q. State whether or not you removed any mortar from the joints in the brick-work and examined it with respect to its quality?

A. I did, sir, in a great many places.

Q. State whether or not you found that mortar satisfactory with respect to quality?

A. I found the mortar, where it had opportunity to dry, a very fine cement.

Q. How was it on the interior of the wall, inward from the outer surface?

A. Improving in some places. I found it was soft and damp.

Q. State whether or not that will improve with age and become set?

A. As soon as the mortar can be dried it will carbonize and become harder each year for twenty years.

Q. State whether or not you gave to the examination of the mortar sufficient attention to say emphatically that the mortar used in these brick walls is generally of good quality?

A. I am very fully satisfied from my examination, which was very thorough, that it is of excellent quality.

Q. State whether or not you examined the sand on the State House grounds or any sand used in making this mortar, and if so what you found its quality to be?

A. I examined several piles of sand around the State House which I found to be of very good quality.

Q. State whether or not it is sharp sand?

A. It is sharp sand.

Q. State whether or not you examined the lime that was used in mixing the mortar?

A. I had no opportunity of examining the lime.

Q. Do you know the Lemont lime?

A. No, sir, I am not familiar with it. I only judge from the mortar that I saw and examined that it must have been good lime.

Q. State whether or not the walls, in their present condition in that building, are of sufficient strength to justify their continuation upward some forty or fifty feet, as is contemplated in the completion of the new State House?

A. The principal walls—yes, sir. There are some of the interior walls where a few courses will have to be taken off the top where the joints have been destroyed by the action of the weather?

Q. State whether or not it will be necessary to remove any of those walls entirely, or any portion of them except a few courses on top?

A. I think I stated that only a few courses on the top would have to be removed from the top downward.

Q. Something has been said about the walls beneath the large openings upon each side of the corridor. State whether or not it is necessary that these walls should be of the best masonry ?

A. I should think the damage to that part of the wall would have no effect upon the strength of the building at all. They appear to be dwarf walls. I don't know what they are for. They might as well have been wood as brick. They give no additional strength to the building, and if taken down would have no effect upon the building.

Q. You spoke awhile ago of the rustic joints, saying you would prefer to have the joints upon the lower surface of the rustic. State now particularly why you would so prefer it ?

A. My attention was called to the rustic joints, some of the joints being at the top and some at the bottom. It makes no difference whether they are upon the top or bottom. I would prefer to have them at the bottom because they could not be seen there.

Q. Is there any reason why the joints should be more favored in these rustics than at other places in the building?

A. There might be less reason because the joint in the rustic is partly protected by the projecting stone above.

Q. State whether or not those stone have been properly cut in all respects, and well set so far as you examined them ?

A. I examined that part of the work, the setting, very critically. I think I never saw a building set more perfectly in line both in perpendicular and lineal.

Q. Are the joints in the stone work sufficiently close ?

A. They are very close and very perfect.

Q. Something has been said with reference to wooden wedges being placed in parts of the stone wall. State whether the placing of those wedges or strips was necessary, and if necessary, what purpose they subserved?

A. It is very often done in setting stone to allow the mortar joints to set, otherwise the stone would drop and press the mortar out. The wedges do no damage whatever. They are taken out after the mortar hardens.

Q. Are the joints in that stone work, so far as you have examined it, good, perfect joints?

A. Yes, sir, I was very much pleased with the joint work. I don't remember a defect that I saw in any part of the stone work.

Q. Will the brick walls in that building support the superstructure necessary for the completion of the building ?

A. I have no doubt of it, sir, to any reasonable hight.

By Mr. Fuller ?

Q. You spoke of the walls remaining wet and every course being grouted, state if you examined the walls to see that for yourself, or whether it is a matter of information ?

A. It is by information. I saw evidences of the grouting upon the side of the wall also.

Q. With reference to the building of brick walls of this kind, is it prudent to build walls of that character during the winter time in this climate ?

A. I should prefer to build them in summer or fall.

Q. Do you think those walls have been injured by the weather ?

A. Not materially, sir.

By Mr. McMillan :

Q. Will it be necessary to remove any of the brick work forming the backing to the stone work ?

A. I don't think I saw any defect in the backing of the cut stone work ?

By Mr. Webb :

Q. State whether or not those walls inside are not in a better condition for plastering on now than if they were pointed up ?

A. I don't think that makes much difference.

Q. Does not the plastering fill up the points in place of pointing ?

A. Yes sir ; it is a mere matter of appearance.

JOHN M. VAN OSDEL.

THIRD DAY.

Friday Evening, *April* 14, 1871.

Thos. W. Brady, examined.

Direct—by Mr. Roberts :

Q. Please state your name, age and place of residence.

A. Thomas W. Brady, 45 years of age, and live at St. Louis.

Q. How long have you lived there?

A. Twenty years.

Q. What is your business?

A. Architect, builder and superintendent.

Q. How long have you been thus engaged?

A. Twenty-five years.

Q. You may state whether you have examined the walls in the new State House?

A. Yes, sir, I have examined them this afternoon. I went through the whole building and examined inside the walls in a great many places—that is, the walls above the basement proper.

Q. Above the cellar?

A. Yes.

Q. State the result.

A. Well, I would much rather give an opinion on that building in about three months from now, than to-day, because the most of that work was put up in winter, in a bad season, and a man hasn't a chance to see the effect which dry weather would have on the mortar.

Q. State your opinion as it appears to-day.

A. The mortar in a thick wall, of course, won't dry as soon as in a thin wall, but there may be another cause of its not drying soon in this case, and that is, the use of that yellow sand, which I think is not fit for buiding purposes.

Q. You examined to see how the mortar was made? I mean the sand out of which it was made?

A. Yes, sir.

Q. State what kind of sand it is.

A. Well, it is what I generally find to be this yellow, decomposed sand—a great deal of loam in it, and matter that will decay or be of no use whatever. The gray sand that I saw there, however, is very good sand, and very well adapted for building purposes, but the other is not good, and I wouldn't use it in any part of brick work or plaster.

Q. Did you examine the lime?

A. I saw some lime run out there, and put a piece of it in my pocket; here it is, (exhibiting a cube of slacked lime about two inches thick,) that has been slacked and run out into what we call a "putty," and that, of course, becomes useless in its present condition.

Q. State what the character of that lime is.

A That lime, used right, would make a very good cement; that's my of it opinion now, from the time I've had to examine it. But I think to let it lie there—I think that it is useless for all purposes.

Q. What is the usual practice regarding to slacking lime, before putting it into a wall?

A. Well, in St. Louis, for all our regular mortar, the lime is made up, run out and used the same day.

Q. How long do you slack the lime beforehand?

A. The sand is on the ground, and the day the work is commenced the lime is brought on the ground and allowed to slack, and then it is piled up and the next day mixed and tempered according to what is needed, and no more is used than is tempered.

Q. What proportion of lime and sand do you use in constructing walls?

A. The regular proportion of mortar is one part lime to two parts sand.

Q. How long does it take that lime and sand mortar to dry and form a cement in walls such as these?

A. That depends a good deal upon the time of year when it was put into the building. Done in winter it will, of course, take a longer time—it will take six months; it must get the use of a dry season to season it—the same as timber as has to go through heat and cold in order to be seasoned—and then it will be longer in a thick wall in proportion to the thickness of it.

Q. Well, in walls that have been laid from July to November? Please state the time it would take them to dry.

A. Well, a nine inch wall or a thirteen inch wall—they ought to be dried out by that time. If it were a thicker wall it might take a longer time.

Q. [To one of the Commissioners.] I believe some of those walls were built in July?

MR. BEVERIDGE:

No, sir; none of them as soon as that; some of them built along in August.

Q. [To the witness.] Well, of walls built last August, what ought to be the condition?

A. That is the worst time to dry, because it is just leading into winter. It would require the next coming summer to season the wall.

Q. I will get you to state, if you went into those walls and examined the mortar, and if you did, state in what condition you found it.

A. I found the mortar tempered and fresh looking.

Q. What is your opinion about its cementing properties? state whether it has cemented or ever will.

A. That is the reason I should prefer to see that mortar, to give a decided opinion, in two or three months from now, because I don't think it has had a fair test; then I could tell whether this loamy sand was in it or not, because if it didn't begin to grow hard from this out, during the dry weather, I know there must be some bad material that may prevent it all the time.

Q. What is your judgment now?

A. I would say that it would cement—that would be my first impression.

Q. The walls—your opinion whether they are good or not?

A. The walls are well built—straight—they are evenly built. The work is very well executed, and the only opinion I could give about it would amount to the same thing.

Q. Did you examine the top courses on those walls?

A. I did. I was on the top and saw where the cement was spread over the walls. They were all covered with a coating and of course the water got down in them, and must have damaged the walls considerably—down three, four or five courses, may be.

Q. Did you examine to see if they were properly grouted?

A. Yes; I found the joints all full of material.

Q. What is the character of the brick?

A. Well, they are not the best brick—at least those that I found there loose, around. They are not as good brick as we have in St. Louis. They are better than some, and worse than others.

Q. Did you think that they were strong enough to bear the pressure that would be required?

A. I think they are sufficiently strong.

Q. State if you examined the stone work.

A. Yes, sir. The stone work, as a whole, is a pretty fair job. Some joints not as close as is usual to make them, and some of the work not cut exactly as I should like. Some of the joints where the arch strikes and forms an angle, instead of the arch meeting the joint straight, it curves out, and will require to be gone over and repaired. I found some of the stone work pieced, and I found one of the sills nearly cracked through.

Q. What is the cause?

A. I should say on account of not being properly set, so that the weight coming on it, pressed down and burst it.

Q. Have you examined the rustics?

A. Yes, I saw them. I would prefer them joined at the top. Though, as it is, I don't look on it as a fatal defect. It would be a better job the other way.

Q. State just the best way of laying stone—cutting the rustic on the bottom or top.

A. I prefer to have the joints as I said, because then there is no chance for leakage.

Q. Will you state if you saw any wooden wedges in under any of the stone there?

A. Yes. I think I saw a few in the cornices, in one or two places.

Q. State what it is done for, and if it is proper.

A. It was done to bring up the level, in case a stone was set on that was slack, and wouldn't exactly fit. The only defect about that, is that it leaves a large joint with no bond, but it don't weaken the building any.

Q. What is the most approved way of doing the work?

A. I think that way ought to be avoided.

By Mr. McMillan:

Q. Will you state, if you please, if you have examined similar walls to these, at the same time after they were built as these?

A. I don't know whether they were exactly the same thickness or not. I've examined the general run of walls, and have seen them at every stage during their building.

Q. In what condition did you find the mortar in any such walls?

A. Sometimes dry and other times damp, according to the length of time.

Q. When you found it damp, then you found the mortar in the same condition you found this mortar?

A. The same appearance—it had the same appearance.

Q. Is there any way of deciding, any time since the mortar was used, whether or not it was good?

A. I would not say, because, as I said before, I would prefer to have two or three dry months come to test by the weather.

Q. Will you state whether or not this mortar has received any injury from exposure to the weather?

A. It has received the injury that all mortar generally will receive. You can take a scale off the outside.

Q. State whether it is a permanent injury.

A. It isn't.

Q. State whether, in your opinion, those walls are sufficient after removing three or four of the top courses, to receive forty or fifty feet more of wall upon them.

A. I would not like to state that positively at the present time of year.

Q. Your opinion is all I ask.

A. I would rather take time to consider that, because, as I said before, I could give it nearly accurately after two or three months.

Q. You may state your opinion with as much reservation as you think proper.

A. I would be inclined to say that they are strong enough to receive two or three stories. I will say that much.

Q. That isn't any definite expression.

A. I don't know what is required to go on top of the walls.

Q. Fifty or sixty feet more. Say whether those walls are sufficiently strong to receive fifty or sixty feet more of wall.

A. Well, I am hardly prepared to answer that, positively. I would say they are. I don't give it as my positive opinion.

Q. State, Mr. Brady, how deep your examinations were made.

A. About two bricks, in about a brick and a half.

Q. State whether or not, to that depth, the mortar hadn't been more injured by weather than it had further down into the wall —whether so or not.

A. Do you mean the top of the wall, or the side? As far as I went the weather affected it, but the effect was getting slighter. Of course, the effect on the top was deeper than on the sides.

Q. Did you see into the walls on the side or top further than the water penetrated?

A. I did.

Q. State whether or not you found the mortar in better condition in that part than you did nearer the surface.

A. I found the mortar damper inside than outside.

Q. State whether or not the mortar was in better condition so as to crystalize and become binding.

A. It was binding.

Q. Was it in a condition to become binding?

A. Yes. I answered a while ago that question.

Q. State whether or not the bricks are good.

A. They are good brick.

Q. Did you find that the work had been done in a workman-like manner?

A. I did. I found the wall was well put up.

By Mr. Roberts:

Q. Let him answer, would it be necessary to take any of those walls down before they go on and build upon them?

A. I think it would be desirable to take four or five courses out of the top all around.

Q. Did you notice any other portions of the walls that it would be necessary to rebuild?

A. No, sir.

By Mr. Webb:

Q. One question in that connection: Any building standing through the winter, built at the time this was, state whether or not it would be necessary to take out three, or four, or five courses.

A. It would when not carefully covered from the weather.

By Mr. Fuller:

Q. Just a question or two: You say that you think it would become hard—if it is good mortar it will become hard by time. Now, what would be the effect upon mortar that was exposed to the air? Would it harden the same that it would in the wall?

A. If it was exposed it will dry quicker.

Q. In the same manner out of the wall as in the wall?

A. It takes more time to harden in the wall, because it hasn't the action of the air upon it.

Q. Would it become just as hard in the air as in the wall, when it was dry?

A. It will—no difference—when it gets time to harden and dry clear through.

Q. If a portion of that was taken out carefully, not disturbed, and dried in the air, would it then become as hard ?

A. Taken out of the wall in the state it is now, I don't think it would.

Q. If it could be removed ?

A. If you got it in a block the same that brick rests on, it would dry just the same.

Q. Would it be in just the same condition out, as in the wall ?

A. Yes, sir.

[Mr. Fuller here exhibited a specimen about two inches square and one-third of an inch thick, and crumbled it upon the table.]

Q. I will just ask, now, whether that mortar is good mortar—whether it is as firm as mortar should be laid in a wall ?

A. It don't appear to be. I think there is a good deal of yellow sand in that.

Q. State whether you think mortar of that character in a wall would make a good wall—a sufficient wall for a building of that kind.

A. It don't appear to have a very good bond there. I don't think that is very good mortar—hasn't a good bond.

By Mr. Roberts :

Q. Would that ever make good mortar, if it was in a wall fresh, and stayed in there ?

A. Well, I couldn't say that. It is mighty hard to tell about mortar. It takes a long time, in some mortar, especially the mortar that is made from lime. It takes longer to set one kind than another.

Q. I will ask you if mortar such as that would have good and sufficient binding qualities to make a good wall ?

A. It hasn't now, but I don't think that is a good specimen to try it by ; because the best mortar in the world, if you take it out from the bottom of a brick, it will break out that way ; whereas, in a bed under the brick, it is getting all the time greater force and power.

By Mr. Fuller :

[To the rest of the Committee]. I will just state, I went over to the building and took a brick out where the wall was solid ; didn't appear to be affected by the weather any more than it is everywhere. I took out several pieces, larger than that ; some of of them very carefully, not to disturb them, and took them up to my room, and laid them down and dried them in the shade. Didn't expose them to either heat or sunshine. That is the specimen, as it is there.

By Mr. Webb:

[To Mr. Fuller]. From one of the top courses?

By Mr. Fuller:

[To Mr. Webb]. No, sir; it was about the depth of six courses. Down below one of the openings where the wall is solid and good. I wouldn't take it from any other place, because my desire was to get a fair sample of the mortar.

Cross-examination by Mr. Webb.—I want to ask you, Mr. Brady, if the brick were wet at the time, if the mortar wouldn't be a longer time in drying?

A. It would, of course, because the brick wouldn't absorb the wet of the mortar so quick.

Q. So as to dry them? That is the object of wetting the brick?

A. It is. To prevent them in very hot weather; because it spoils the bond if the wet is taken up too quick.

Q. I understand you that this work, if done at the time mentioned, along in August, you couldn't tell at this time whether the mortar is good or not, until it has gone through a season?

A. I said I preferred in giving an answer in two or three months.

Q. Well, I will ask you another question: If the mortar was damp in the walls?

A. It is.

Q. Then, if that mortar was taken out and dried in twenty-four hours, exposed to the sun or a hot room, or the weather so as to dry in twenty-four hours, would it be of the same quality?

A. It would not be as good, because it wouldn't be taking a proper time to season.

Q. From seeing mortar that has been dried, taken out of the wall in the condition you find it there (pointing to the specimen on the table), could you tell whether the mortar in the walls is good or not?

A. I could not. I said so.

Q. If the mortar had been dried the same as that showed by Mr. Fuller, under the process he spoke of, and if it had the appearance it has here, how would that mortar likely be, if it dried in the walls?

A. It might be good if the sand is all right. It will improve if the sand is all right.

Q. Would it not be far superior to have that dried in the air, as stated?

A. It would. You can never test mortar that way with regard to its bond.

Q. You spoke about the lime. Do you know whether the lime, in the condition found, was used in the walls or not?

A. I don't know.

Q. You spoke of that (pointing to the cube of slacked lime), as if we might judge from that.

A. I didn't mention it at all in connection with the walls.

Q. You were asked about the lime, in what condition it is.

A. I said I found some of it that way, and said it is useless now.

Q. Then you don't know that the lime was used in that condition?

A. No, sir.

Q. You don't know, but that lime, before it was in that condition, was good?

A. I do not.

Q. Do you know the Lemont lime?

A. No.

Q. I will ask you if you hav'nt been in the habit of working the white sand or Mississippi sand?

A. We use the Mississippi sand for all the houses we build.

Q. Have you ever used this yellow sand?

A. No—never.

Q. Have you ever had any practical experience of it?

A. I see it in parts of the country outside of St. Louis. I think it is what we call a kind of sand that is mixed with clay. It is found in all sandstone quarries.

Q. Do you know it is the same thing?

A. Much the same. I should say the same.

Q. Did you examine it particularly?

A. I did. I looked very close. I wouldn't use that sand in any building I have been putting up.

Q. Well, I will ask you if the kind of sand you examined then, this yellow sand, was one of the parts of that mortar exhibited there. Can you say, that if it had been left in the walls and allowed to dry, by the time it had dried it wouldn't make good mortar?

A. I don't think it would ever make a good bond. That is my opinion.

Q. I understood you to say that the work was well done?

A. It is well built; laid up evenly; the walls straight and level.

Q. I believe you stated in your direct examination that those walls were made so they would be suitable on which to build a structure some sixty feet high.

A. That is the appearance of them to me.

Q. From your examination?

A. That is, as I said before. I would not like to give a positive opinion just now. It is a doubtful affair with me, at present.

Q. I will ask you how that could be safe, and the mortar made out of the sand you examined; if that kind of sand has gone into those walls—if the mortar used in those walls has been made from that sand with lime—if it has been made from that sand, how can you say that it would be good for a structure some sixty feet high?

A. Well, if it was made out of that sand entirely, I would not risk to say it.

Q. Did you find the mortar when you examined the walls thus erected—at the time they were laid, and having undergone the effects of the weather during the winter—did you find them as you expected?

A. Exposed as they were, they were as good as I need expect to find them. I didn't expect to find them thoroughly dried.

Q. Then the condition of the mortar being damp and moist there, is it any evidence that when they should have stayed some three or four months longer, during warm weather; is it any evidence that the mortar is not good?

A. It is not.

THOMAS W. BRADY.

(Signed by the reporter as directed by the witness.)

CORNELIUS PRICE.

Examined by Mr. McMillan:

Q. What is your name, age, occupation and place of residence?

A. Cornelius Price; occupation, builder; residence, Chicago, and age, fifty years.

Q. How long have you been engaged in building?

A. About thirty years.

Q. What character of builder do you mean—carpenter or mason work?

A. Mason work.

Q. State whether or not you have examined the new capitol building at this place?

A. I have.

Q. State as fully and as briefly as you can the result of that examination.

A. The first examination I made was in the basement or lower part of the basement story, which I examined very thoroughly. I found the work in a very good condition there; the brick and arches laid in cement. Then I examined the story above the brick work and stone work both. I found a portion of the upper story laid in water lime, commonly called cement mortar. I found that also in good condition. I also examined the execution of the work. I found the work very properly executed, the walls plumb and straight. I examined that portion of the building laid up in what is called Athens mortar, made by lime said to contain cement qualities. I found that mortar soft—the outside of it. I examined the outside part thoroughly, and found some of it frozen, or had been frozen and had scaled off. I got a chisel then and hammer and cut into the interior of the wall, and examined it then. I found the mortar in better condition in them than upon the outside, although the wall was very damp. I attributed that, to a considerable extent, to the walls being left exposed all winter, and not having been properly cared for. I found the work laid very well—well grouted, the joints well filled in the interior walls. I did not cut into the outside walls. I found lime was used of that character all over the building. I examined the north and south sides. On the south exposure I found the mortar a little harder than upon the north exposure, because the sun shining upon it dried it out more.

Q. State what kind of material was used in making the mortar in which the brick work, of which you have spoken, was made

A. I noticed a portion of it, the corridor walls, were laid in cement water lime principally, no mixture of quick lime in it. It was in very good condition, except a few courses on the top.

Q. The question is as to what kind of material.

A. I am speaking of the material. It was laid in water lime, free from quick lime; the north and south flank, I think, was laid up in quick lime, Lemont or Athens lime. That mortar had not become hard.

Q. My question is as to the character of the materials used in making that mortar—speak of the sand and lime of which it was made.

A. I did not see the lime, only as it was mixed with the mortar put into the building. I saw some of it slacked and left out exposed, but I saw nothing of the lime, except as it was mixed; I suppose the mortar was properly mixed with that red sand.

Q. What kind of sand was used in making this mortar?

A. I should think the largest portion was red sand, taken out of the river line.

Q. Is that such sand as you would denominate sharp sand?

A. Yes, sir; it is quite sharp. It is not the best quality of sand.

Q. Is it a good quality of sand?

A. It is good of the kind.

Q. Is it a good quality of sand?

A. I have never called it first quality of sand; they have two or three large piles of gray sand there, that is good sand.

Q. Still you do not answer the question as to whether that is good sand.

A. The gray sand is good; the other sand I said was not first quality.

Q. Is it a good quality?

A. It is, so far that I think very good mortar can be made out of it.

Q. State, whether or not you know the Lemont lime.

A. I have never used any lime properly coming from there; I have used the Lockport lime.

Q. Do you know whether or not that is made of the same quality of stone?

A. All I know about the Lockport lime is, that I used it in —— buildings, and found it was not quick lime; it would slack, but in slacking it didn't increase in bulk—I could put it all back in the same barrel; it made a good strong wall. It is a lime I do not use, because it is not profitable. It don't make as much mortar as lime we have in Chicago.

Q. State whether or not the walls in this new building are in good condition?

A. I should not say that those walls, laid up with that quick lime, are in good condition—not on account of the mortar used, but more on account of the manner they have been cared for. There is neglect of duty on some ones' part, in not properly taking care of the walls.

Q. State whether or not those walls are defective, from the want of proper materials from which the mortar was made.

A. I think, probably, the material was good; that the mortar was good if the building had been properly taken care of, and not been left exposed to the weather until it destroyed the outside surface of the mortar—that part exposed to view in the joints. Upon further examination into the walls, I found the frost had not affected it.

Q. State whether or not the mortar in new walls will improve by age and become adhesive.

A. I think it will; all that has not been destroyed by frost, which extends probably an inch into the wall, will become hard. I think the interior of the walls will get hard.

Q. State from the condition in which you found these walls, whether, in your opinion, they ought to be taken down and rebuilt.

A. I do not think it is necessary to tear down the walls and re-build them; probably they will have to take off two or three feet from the top, and rebuild that.

Q. State whether or not those walls are sufficient, in their present condition, to admit of their extension upwards, some forty to sixty feet, after taking off the courses you spoke of.

A. I think they would be sufficient.

Q. Can you state, then, when the walls are completed, whether they would be entirely safe and endurable?

A. Yes, sir, I think they would be. I will give you a little idea about mortar setting. In Chicago we frequently build walls up in ninety days; I built the Tremont House, in Chicago, in that way; the mortar in the construction of it had not time to dry and set; it was probably just as green in the interior of the walls, when completed, as when we commenced building it; the walls were some eighty or ninety feet high, and there was no bond to the mortar all the time; it became set afterwards. It is a principle, that the longer the walls stand the harder the mortar becomes; there is no time fixed when it will become set and stop cementing. I don't know as I have ever read any work upon mortar, stating the time when it will stop cementing and growing harder.

Q. State whether, or not, that is a first class job of brick work?

A. So far as the execution of the work is concerned, it is first class.

Q. I speak of the material used in its construction, also.

A. The material used may be different from the material I find there now. I find the walls being so exposed that the material has been injured, to a certain extent, by exposure to the weather.

Q. State whether, or not, it is possible to make a first class job of that building, without tearing down these walls?

A. Yes sir, I think it will make a good building, without tearing down the walls.

Q. Will it be a first class job, when completed?

A. I should think they could make a first class job, after taking off a few feet of those walls and building it up again. It will make a first class job. In two or three months the mortar in those walls will be very different from what it is now.

Q. Is it possible to make a first quality of mortar unless you use first quality material, including both lime and sand?

A. No, sir; I don't think you can make a first class quality of anything out of an inferior article.

Q. Could you make first quality of mortar out of the sand you found upon the State House ground?

A. Out of that grey sand I could; sand I understand they got out of the Illinois river.

Q. Could you make first class mortar out of the yellow sand you found upon the ground there?

A. No, sir; it is not a first quality of sand.

Q. Do you know whether that yellow sand was used in making the mortar you examined to day, in that building?

A. I only know what the superintendent said about it. I asked him which sand the walls were laid up with; he said it was laid up in about equal proportions. I could not tell by examining the mortar, as the color of the sand was changed by the lime.

Q. Would the mixture of the two kinds of sand you speak of, with the proper proportion of lime, make a first quality of mortar?

A. It would make a good quality, but not first class. It is out of the nature of things to make first class mortar out of that red sand. We have sand upon the lake that makes first class mortar. It is sand, with no impure substance in it.

Q. State anything further you know with reference to the material used in that building?

A. I have never used the Lemont lime. All I know of it is what the maker of it has told me. I made objections to his lime on account of the cement water lime in it. It sets very quick, and we could not work it with ease.

By Mr. Roberts:

Q. State if you examined the stone work, the cut stone work upon that building?

A. I did.

Q. State your opinion about that.

A. I found some defects in the cutting of it, in some of the joints, but upon the whole I think it is a very good job. I will say this that I was surprised that so good a job could come from the State Prison.

Q. Is it a first class job of stone work?

A. It approaches very near first class. In cutting so large an amount of stone there must necessarily be some stone that would be marred. It has been handled with considerable care, and it is well set.

Cross examination by Mr. Webb, on behalf of the Commissioners:

Q. You say that Lemont lime is unprofitable. You mean it is unprofitable to the contractor?

A. Yes sir.

Q. I believe you did not state that you had knowledge as to whether it was good lime?

A. No, sir; I never used it. The maker of it has very frequently offered to send some of it to me to let me test it, but I never used any of it.

Q. Taking the brick work and stone work together, what would you say as to the quality of it as a whole?

A. It is just as I have stated. The only defect is that the mortar being soft it has been exposed too much to the weather, but the work is well executed.

Q. The mortar in the interior, as I understand you, will harden?

A. It is better there than upon the outside of the walls. I think it will become hard in time. It will probably be wet inside there for two years; the mortar the most exposed will of course harden first:

By Mr. FULLER, on direct examination:

Q. State whether such a mixture of sand as you spoke of, when hardened with age, will the mortar be of a suitable quality for the erection of such a building as that?

A. Yes sir; I think it will make the walls sufficiently hard to carry the building, but it does not make as good mortar as we have at Chicago, I think.

By Mr. ROBERTS:

Q. Do you know what proportion of lime, cement and sand was used in the mixture of this mortar?

A. I could tell nothing about it from the examination of the mortar. I asked the superintendent if there was any cement mixed in the mortar or whether they relied upon the cement in the lime. He said he relied entirely upon the cement in the lime; that he did not mix any cement with the mortar.

Q. State whether that was likely to make as good mortar as called for in these specifications, which reads as follows:

"All brick walls above to be laid with mortar composed of one part of cement, one part of lime slacked at least one week before using, and five parts of clean sharp sand?"

A. They have got it very indefinite in that specification, but they must have construed it that the lime must be slacked and sand put into it before using some time, as I found a large amount of slacked lime laying there that is entirely useless. As regards the properties of cement in this lime I know nothing about it.

Q. Would it make good mortar the way the superintendent stated to you they mixed the mortar?

A. I think it would make better mortar the way it is specified there in the specification. The proper way to use cement in mortar made of quick lime is to make it as you want to use it. When you come to mix up ready to lay brick, the proper way would be to mix the cement through the mortar as it is used. It should all be used the day it is mixed ; cement after it once begins to set, and is then broken up, is useless.

CORNELIUS PRICE.

THURSDAY EVENING, *May* 25, 1871.

BOWLIN-STARCK, examined.

The witnesses to-day were sworn.

BY MR. ROBERTS :

Q. What is your name?

A. Bowlin-Starck.

Q. You may state if, at any time, you have made any measurement of the brick in the new State House, and if so at what time, and what the result of that measurement was.

A. At your request, I started about one week before the last adjournment to measure the brick work. I stayed afterward and finished the measurement.

Q. State whether you measured in accordance with the specifications, and how much you made it out to be.

A. I made six million two hundred and fifty thousand.

Q. State where those brick were.

A. In the upper walls, in the cellar, and the arches. I don't refer to the outside, at all—only the bricks used in the building.

BY MR. EAGAN :

Q. Does the amount of brick include ——

A. The brick laid in the walls and cellar and are called basement story—the whole building as far as finished.

BY MR. ROBERTS :

Q. State whether that is kiln measurement or not.

A. It is measurement in accordance with the specifications. When I measured these walls I had first to ascertain the result by both ways—first by kiln measurement and then according to specifications, without allowing the deductions made in the arches, and run in I believe with the kiln brick about five millions—the actual bricks laid in the walls.

Q. Did you show your manner of measuring to any other architects or builders—and if so, to whom?

A. In the first place, the assistant, Mr. Clark I asked him how he would measure, and he informed me. Mr. Piquenard I asked, and he informed me about some measurement there. For instance, the air ducts and air flues, according to Mr. Clark's statement to me, he had measured them solid. Mr. Piquenard told me they should not be measured solid. The smoke flues were measured solid, but the others were not.

Q. State whether the specifications required them thus to be measured solid.

A. The specifications, as I understand, provides for them not to be measured solid.

Q. Have you shown your figures to any other architects or builders?

A. I have shown them to Mr. Boyington, Mr. Wheelock, Mr. Carter and Mr. Loring.

Cross examined by Mr. McMillan.—I will get you to explain particularly the manner of brick measurement made by you on this building.

A. I made it according to specifications. The specification calls for one brick and a half in length, being one foot; that gives the thickness of the wall. Then, after getting the cubic contents of the wall, it is to be multiplied by twenty-one, because one cubic foot requires twenty-one brick.

Q. Did you include the openings in the flues?

A. I have excluded all openings, except the spring of the arch; from the spring of the arch that is measured solid.

Q. What arches do you speak of—those above the opening in the wall, or those which are to serve as the foundation of the basement floor.

A. All.

Q. Did you measure the contents of every wall in that building?

A. I did.

Q. Was your measurement taken from the measurement of those walls as they appeared there, or from plans and specifications?

A. From the walls as they appeared.

Q State in what manner you measured that part of the brick-work which interlaces with the stone.

A. That is only in the outside wall. I had to make an average.

Q. Is it not true that the stone in the outside wall are of different thicknesses.

A. Certainly ; every other course is different.

Q. Was it possible that you could have made an accurate measurement of brick work where it joins the stone work ?

A. Near enough for every practical purpose. Because, if you allow me to make a diagram, a section of that outside wall would look this way: [A diagram was shown by witness.] Now I have tried, as near as possible, to get an average of this.

Q. According to your explanation, one course of this stone is receding. Is there any uniformity ?

A. I could not answer that; there may be a few inches of variation.

Q. Can you say there is any material difference ?

A. I don't believe there is any material difference.

Q. Please state your rule for ascertaining the cubical contents of a section of sphere.

A. You have to get the area of the sphere and multiply it.

Q. Give your rule.

Mr. Roberts:

I don't know what that has to do with the case. We are all going to get into a fog.

Q. I just wish to ask the gentleman for information to ascertain his qualifications as a measurer. State, if you please, what is your rule for ascertaining the cubical contents of an arch.

A. According to the specifications, they are to be measured solid, from the spring of the arch.

Q. Does that mean to its base ? To what point ?

A. Up. For instance here (illustrating), measured from the base up solid.

Q. These arches having all been formed in the basement floor, how was it possible for you to measure the spring of the arch ?

A. Well, having first got the whole solid, from the floor to the foundation, then from the foundation—the spring of the arch—it is easy enough to measure to the crown of the arch; that gives me the whole of it.

Q. Did you apply that rule in all your measurement ?

A. In all my measurement of the basement arches.

Q. Was the floor of the basement of uniform level?

A. The foundations are of uniform level; there might be a few little variations, but no material difference; I have discovered none in the basement. There are some little seams in the floor in some places.

Q. Well, sir, what do your figures show the number of brick to have been?

A. Six millions two hundred and fifty thousand.

Q. How many of those brick were in the basement, and how many in the four walls?

A. I have it in my papers, but they are not here now. The proportion I don't recollect.

Q. If you have made any calculation will you submit it as part of your testimony?

A. I would if I had it here; I have it on slips of paper. I can make it out and attach it here.

Mr. Roberts:

You may do so.

By Mr. Robinson, Commissioner:

Q. I believe I understand, Mr. Starck, that you have all your calculations—all your figures?

A. Yes, sir, I believe I have.

Q. Will you be kind enough to tell the committee how long you were engaged in measuring that work?

A. I was first engaged about seven or eight days before the House adjourned, then after they adjourned, I was, perhaps, three or four days longer; though I don't mean to say I was there the whole day.

Q. About how long were you up there?

A. In the beginning, I was there a long time, because I wanted to hurry the thing, and get the measurement finished before the House adjourned; but as I could'nt accomplish it at the time, afterwards I didn't stay so long.

Q. Who assisted you?

A. A young man engaged in my office—a draughtsman.

Q. What's his name?

A. His name is Weldon; they call him Tom.

Q. Who made your calculations?

A. Myself; nobody assisted me.

Q. Let me ask you, have you ever seen the calculations and figures of Mr. Clark?

A. No, sir; never have.

Q. Do you know what the thickness of the walls is?

A. I have not seen his figures.

Q. How have you measured?

A. I started to measure from the west—southwest room, and then I went round.

Q. Will your figures show the thickness of all the outside walls around?

A. Certainly, except the stone.

Q. How do you know how thick those walls are? Tell the committee how you could estimate the brick there.

A. We had that here a few minutes ago—the same thing. Some parts of the stone are exposed, and I measured the thickness of them and I have averaged the whole.

Q. You didn't, in any place, go through the wall?

A. I did not knock a hole through the wall. The main walls I could judge of, easily enough. Those composed of stone and brick had to be averaged.

Q. You had to guess at the figures, did you not?

A. Had to do the best I could. Measured as far as I could without knocking a hole through the wall.

Q. When you got down in the cellar, the specifications required you to measure from the spring of the arch to the top, making it all solid. How could you tell? How could you tell how far it was—how deep the arches went?

A. I reckoned from the floor above to the foundation; from the basement floor, the whole hight of the cellar.

Q. I want to see how much experience you have. Now, here is the spring of the arch (illustrating). Now, sir, how could you tell, when the floor was all over there, how far it was up from the spring to the top—no hole to see through?

A. (Witness illustrating.) Suppose here is the arch, and there the spring of the arch. I know how far it is from here to here, and from that I get the thickness of the floor. (Some further illustrations were not clear to the reporter.)

Q. Mr. Starck, I want to have the committee learn something about your ability to measure. Have you had large experience in measuring brick walls?

A. I have measured some.

Q. What is your profession?

A. Civil engineering.

[MR. ROBERTS.—I would say, that in the original examination witness gave a complete history of his life.]

[MR. ROBINSON.—I think there are some things that perhaps he hasn't given. I know something about the gentleman's history.]

(To the witness.)

Q. How long have you been in this country?

A. Fifteen years.

Q. Where have you worked?

A. Both New York and Philadelphia.

Q. How long in Philadelphia?

A. From 1863 till two years ago.

Q. Just give the names of the men you worked for in Philadelphia.

A. Mr. Samuel Sloan was one; Mr. John McArthur. They were the two principal architects I worked for. Then I had an office of my own. I worked for the United States--for General Crossman. That's in Philadelphia.

Q. What is Sloan's profession?

A. He is an architect.

Q. Is he a man of ability in his profession?

A. I believe him to be so.

Q. A man of integrity and truth?

A. I believe so.

Q. McArthur an architect?

A. He is. I was employed, at first, with him about four months, and then a short time afterwards I was again employed when he got his large building, the Free Mason's hall. I worked again for him four months.

Q. Was he an architect?

A. Yes, sir.

Q. A man of ability and integrity?

A. Yes, sir.

Q. What other architects did you know. Give some of the principal ones.

A. Several. Mr. Somers is one. Then the principal architect of the Free Mason's hall; I've forgotten his name. Then Fournice and Frazer.

Q. Did you do anything more than drawing?

A. Drawing was a part of my work.

Q. Did you ever get up the plan of a building?

A. Yes.

Q. For Mr. Sloan?

A. For Mr. McArthur, I did. Besides, I got a written statement from some of those gentlemen, and have brought it with me.

Q. I know about your written statements. I understand about your written history. When did you leave there?

A. About two years ago.

Q. Been back there since?

A. Four months after I came here I went back.

Q. How long did you stay?

A. About two weeks.

Q. Been back since?

A. Never.

[COPY.]

PHILADELPHIA, *January* 29, 1869.

The undersigned, at the request of Mr. C. P. Bolin-Starck, take pleasure in recommending him for such employment as he may seek; having been in our employ at various times, we can testify to his being a competent draughtsman, and steady, industrious and intelligent gentleman.

SAMUEL SLOAN, Architect, 152, South Fourth Street, Philadelphia.

W. S. ANDREWS, Architect 209, South Sixth St.

LEWIS COOPER, 2030, Walnut St.

OSCAR F. MOORE, 329, Walnut St.

HENRY CARTWRIGHT, 1st President American Meter Co.

JOSEPH HARRISON.

JAMES O. WATSON, 1229, N. Broad St.

GEO. SUMMERS, Architect, 206, South Sixth St.

G. H. CROSSMAN, A. Q. M., U. S. A., 2014, Delancy Place.

JOHN MCARTHUR, JR., Architect, 209, South Sixth St.

THOS. A. BARLOW.

I concur in the foregoing recommendations.

MORTON MCMICHAEL.

To Whom it may Concern:

We certify that we have employed Mr. C. Starck as a draughtsman, and that we have been satisfied with his work, and that we recommend him to any one who may require the services of a good architectural draughtsman and colorist.

Cochrane & Piquenard, *Architects.*

Springfield, *May* 10, 1870.

Mr. Edward Baker:

We, the undersigned, would most respectfully request that you would appoint Mr. C. Bolin-Starck as draughtsman to make copies of distilleries for your district. Mr. Starck understands this class of work well, having been engaged in this business in Philadelphia. Mr. S. will give you entire satisfaction.

E. E. Myers, *Architect,*
Chas. Fisher,
Edward Rummel,
E. S. Johnson.

Mr. Starck has been well recommended to me as an excellent draughtsman and a worthy, reliable gentleman.

John M. Palmer.

I concur in the foregoing recommendations of Mr. Starck, as a good draughtsman and pleasant gentleman.

Chas. Ridgley.

—

Otis L. Wheelock, sworn:

Questions by Mr. Roberts:

Q. State your name, age and place of residence.

A. My name is Otis L. Wheelock; my residence is Chicago, and my age fifty four.

Q. What is your profession?

A. An architect.

Q. How long have you been engaged in this business?

A. Twenty-five years.

Q. Where?

A. Sixteen years in Chicago; the rest of the time in New York State.

Q. Are you acquainted with Mr. Bolin-Starck—the gentleman who has just testified?

A. I have only seen him to-day.

Q. Have you examined so as to know anything about the manner in which he made the measurement of the brick-work in the new State House?

A. I know by what he showed me—by diagrams—how he arrived at the measurement.

Q. You may state what your judgment is as to the correctness of the measurement.

A. I should say his measurement was very liberal. I should say he figured it a little too much in some instances.

Q. Have you examined the walls?

A. Yes, sir.

Q. State the result of your examination as to the manner in which he measured it, whether it was liberal, and whether he accounted for all the brick there is?

A. I think he counted more brick than there is.

Q. State whether you have ever examined the specifications under which that brick was to be laid?

A. Never very thoroughly; the other gentlemen read it over two or three times in my hearing. We had some discussion on the specification, as to the mode of measuring. It seems the specifications were made when there were not to be any arches, but only iron girders; it was afterwards changed to put in arches, and the mode of measurement was the same comparatively.

Q. State if in your opinion the number of bricks he allows to be as much as the State House probably contains.

A. I think a little more.

Q. I will get you to state, if you have examined the brick-work, as to the manner in which it is laid.

A. I went with the other gentlemen, this morning, quite early, all through the halls and all on top of the walls, and examined pretty thoroughly, perhaps forty or fifty places, and found some walls very good, indeed—mortar pretty hard—other places found pretty bad. I had made up my mind that about half of the walls above the foundation should be taken down.

Q. State your reason for so thinking.

A. The mortar isn't good.

Q. Will it ever make a first class job?

A. I think it never will.

Q. Did you examine? What portion of the walls did you examine?

A. We examined nearly all there was above the basement story.

Q. I will ask you if the defects in those walls wasn't likely to be caused by being exposed to the weather?

A. I should think not.

Q. What experience have you had in regard to construction of walls?

A. If there is a hard frost before the mortar is dry it will injure the mortar.

Q. You may state if you have examined the specifications in regard to the walls, how the brick were to be laid?

A. Yes, sir.

Q. Did they keep within the specifications?

A. I should think the mortar was not.

Q. Have you examined the sand and lime there?

A. Didn't see any lime; examined some sand—some bank sand and some river sand—not as good as our lake shore sand.

Q. State the character of that sand.

A. The largest pile of sand contained considerable loam.

Q. State whether good sand or not.

A. I should think not.

Q. Can there be good work done with it?

A. I should think not first-class work.

Q. You may state, Mr. Wheelock, whether or not this is a first-class job—the brick work on the State House?

A. I should say the brick are well laid.

Q. The balance of the work—the material?

A. The material isn't good.

Q. For making a first-class job?

A. I should think not.

Q. You may state, if you will, what proportion of that work is not good.

A. About one-half above foundation.

Q. Did you examine the foundation?

A. Went down below, but 'twas pretty dark—couldn't tell much about it.

Q. State whether, in your judgment, it would be safe and proper to erect such an extensive and weighty building, as the State House proposes to be, on those walls there?

A. Well, sir, I think it would be preferable to take them down.

Q. Have you examined the plans under which that State House has been erected, and proposes to be finished?

A. I looked them all over in Mr. Piquenard's office, and I could see nothing wrong about the plans. Of course, I couldn't examine critically.

Q. State whether those were the original plans by which the State House was built?

A. I don't know, except what they told about it.

Q. Who told you?

A. Mr. Bolin-Starck; I talked with Mr. Piquenard — not about that being the plan.

Q. Have the plans been changed?

A. Don't know.

Q. Don't know whether they worked according to the original plans or not?

A. Do not; I suppose not from what they told me—this measurer told me.

Q. Did you see the plans?

A. Yes, sir.

Q. Was the work done in accordance with those plans—and the measurement?

A. As far as I could judge.

Q. According to those plans, and the way the work has been done, can you approximate what the building will cost?

A. It will be nothing but guess work.

Q. Your best judgment?

A. We became satisfied among us that we would not dare to state less than six millions. Of course, it would depend largely upon how elaborately the work was done.

Q. In accordance with the plans, and allowing reasonably for the construction, what, in your judgment, will be the probable cost?

A. I wouldn't want to state less than six millions. Of course, I should have you understand the estimate is based somewhat on what has already been paid out.

Q. I will ask you, if you were shown the manner in which this work was measured, whether or not it was measured in the ordinary way of measuring brick work?

A. No, sir; it is more liberal than the usual mode of measuring.

Q. State the usual way.

A. Half openings—take out half openings. In very large openings take out all of them; in very large arches, instead of taking a straight line across the spring of the arch, we would run two lines from the spring of the arch to the center, and take that for the line; instead of taking a line from the spring of the arch—where it was twenty feet, or something like that.

Q. What are the arches there?

A. Twenty feet.

Q. Was it possible to measure those walls, where they butt up against the stone work, with any kind of certainty?

A. I think it is.

Q. State the manner in which they were measured.

A. Mr. Starck told me he was informed those stone were a certain number of inches thick—some more, some less; he took an average of the thickness of the wall, and of the stone, and in that way took a very close average of the brick work.

Q. Could it be measured in that way?

A. I think it could; and if the gentleman has measured in that way, he has measured correctly.

Q. From your conversation with him, what is your opinion of his competency?

A. I should think him very competent.

Questions by Mr. Robinson, Commissioner:

Q. You say that about half those walls should be taken down? Does that include all the cross walls, back up against the stone? Does it include half of any other work?

A. Should think not; I don't remember examining further; it was the partitioning walls—the cross walls—I referred to.

Q. Do you mean, Mr. Wheelock, that they ought to be taken out half way to the basement? Or do you mean that half of the walls should be taken entirely down?

A. Better be taken down to the floor.

Q. Do you think the inside and cross walls are good or bad?

A. Some of those are very good; I should think it is the corner this way—I went 'round that way and went into the west end; went through the building; Mr. Piquenard's office was over on the other end, opposite where we went in; the walls on the left hand side just beyond the dome very good indeed; you may see a very marked difference.

Q. Two pretty large walls?

A. Yes, sir.

Q. That's a pretty fair wall—which one, the large or the small?

A. I should think the large one; the mortar looks very white, very fair.

Q. The other not so good?

A. No, sir.

Q. Is the brick itself good brick?

A. They are not as good brick as we have in Chicago.

Q. You have a pretty good opinion of Chicago, have you? (laughing).

A. Take a Chicago brick and strike it, and it will ring like iron.

Q. Are they good brick for this latitude?

A. I guess they are—I should think so.

Q. The brick appeared to be well laid?

A. Yes, sir.

Q. Right amount of mortar put in?

A. A little more mortar than I should like to see—should like to see a closer joint.

Q. The fault consists in lime and sand, does it?

A. Yes, sir.

Q. Could there be good mortar made out of this lime and sand?

A. I should think not.

Q. Have you used the Lemont lime?

A. I have discarded it altogether.

Q. Don't regard it as good lime?

A. No, sir.

Q. Then the fault, as I understand, is in the mortar, and not in the brick or the work?

A. Yes, sir.

Q. Did you notice the stone work?

A. The foundation stone.

Q. Did you notice the general appearance?

A. Pretty fair work—some of the joints want trimming.

Q. What is it worth to put brick in the wall—parties finding the brick and all the material?

A. I am hardly competent to answer, because I don't know how much your clear sand would cost; I heard somebody else say he made an estimate—he says fourteen dollars a thousand—that's all I could say.

Q. Eleven dollars and fifty cents would be very low, would it not?

A. I should think so.

Q. What was it worth to set those stone?

Mr. ROBERTS:

I suppose, Mr. Robinson, you are lawyer enough to know.

MR. ROBINSON:

I suppose you are no prosecutor. All I want to do is to get at the facts. We have no objections to the truth coming out. [To the witness.]

Q. What was it worth to set the stone?

A. Don't know.

Q. You are an architect, not a builder?

A. No, sir.

Q. Well, is an architect necessarily a good judge of work?

A. He ought to be; I have been a builder.

Q. You have experience. Do you know an architect, Mr. Bauer?

A. Yes, sir.

Q. Do you know Mr. Carter?

A. Yes, sir.

Q. Do you know a builder there by the name of Deekman?

A. Yes, sir.

Q. What is their character?

A. Bauer and Carter are very good.

Q. Deekman's character as a builder?

A. Good as a stone contractor.

Q. Would you have faith in their judgment, as much faith in their estimate, of the cost of a building, as you would have in their being good architects (and Deekman); would you have faith in their estimate and judgment?

A. Yes, sir. Deekman has made several estimates, and finished some contracts in my office.

Q. You say from the diagrams this man here testifying showed you, you judge he gave a very liberal measurement. You know nothing about the measurement?

A. Well, I say he showed me how he arrived at it.

Q. If it should turn out that he had very little capacity, and none for measuring, you would not have very much faith in his results.

A. Well, sir—

Q. You based all your statement about the measurement on what he told you about his plan of measurement. If he didn't tell you the truth you would know nothing?

A. No, sir.

Q. Are you a partner of Mr. Boynton?

A. No, sir. We were together fourteen years, after that we dissolved our partnership. We were together seven or eight years building the penitentiary at Joliet.

Q. Have you been in competition, in any way, for a job, with Piquenard and Cochrane?

A. No, sir.

Q. I only asked; you architects have so much rivalry.

A. Personally, I am a very warm friend of Mr. Cochrane; Mr. Piquenard I never saw until to-day.

Questions by Mr. ROBERTS:

Q. I want to ask you a question. Do you know, of your own knowledge, what it is worth to lay the brick in the wall with the kind of material that have been used here?

A. I do not; a little less than fourteen dollars.

Q. How much less?

A. I suppose a man could lay them for eleven dollars and forty cents.

Q. Do you know what it would be worth to lay first-class work, sand, lime and brick?

A. No, sir.

Q. This Lemont lime, do you know anything about how that rates?

A. Not used at all in Chicago.

Q. For what reason?

A. Bad lime.

Q. Did you observe anything about the bottom arches?

A. I think when you take out your supports they will fall down:

Q. What will be the result?

A. They will fall on the floor below.

Q. What will be the effect on the building?

A. No effect on the building.

Q. What are those arches intended to support?

A. Nothing. I suppose they are only to divide the space; to make an airduct support.

Q. If they fall down, must they be rebuilt again?

A. Yes, sir. The arch is so flat, that it is not more than four inches here [illustrating].

Q. How far across is it?

A. Six or seven feet.

Questions by Mr. ROBINSON, Commissioner:

Q. You say the spring of the arch isn't more than five inches; this flat arch, there isn't a particle of weight on it; it will stand of itself; there is just one row of bricks on it?

A. Yes, sir.

Questions by Mr. BEVERIDGE, Commissioner:

Q. Could it get down without crushing in the brick and mortar?

A. The mortar will have to yield, but I saw no reason why the arch shouldn't have more spring.

By Mr. ROBINSON:

Q. Just now you spoke, in answer to Mr. Roberts, about this work. Don't you suppose a man could do the work with this sand; a man might lose money on it?

A. Yes, sir; our contractors do very frequently.

Q. In your judgment, a good job can't be done with the sand on the ground?

A. Yes, sir; that's what I meant to say.

Q. If you have heard why the lime isn't good, tell why?

A. I don't know, it has been so long since I have had any acquaintance with it.

Q. You don't know but what it is better now than it used to be; but what they are getting it out of an entirely different strata? I understand that to be the fact.

A. No, sir.

Q. You don't know whether it is good now or not?

A. No, sir.

W. W. BOYINGTON, sworn:

Questions by Mr. ROBERTS:

Q. I will get you to state if you know Mr. Bolin-Starck, who measured this State House work?

A. I have known him between one and two years.

Q. Have you had any conversation with him, in which he has explained to you the manner in which he measured this work?

A. He has explained it very fully from the plans, and from the building, and from other demonstrations he made on paper.

Q. State your judgment as to whether it was a correct way of arriving at the measurement.

A. Well, I asked him some particulars—why he made some allowances for certain arches, and he said he said he had done it by taking the construction of the specifications as nearly as he could. I did'nt exactly agree with him in reference to construing the specifications; however, he said he had measured so and so, taking in the arches from the spring of the arch, which in some of them would make a very large measurement, amounting to 300,000 brick.

Q. From your judgment, is he a competent man to make such a measurement as that?

A. He seems to be a man who understands himself very thoroughly, both in measurement and other architectural matters.

Q. Does he seem to understand the general principles by which such work is done?

A. I should think he did, sir, thoroughly.

Q. I will ask you if you have ever made an examination of the plans of this State House, and, if so, when, and to what extent?

A. I examined them to-day, slightly, about an hour or so.

Q. I will ask you if those were the original plans by which the State House—the bricks were laid, so far as they have been laid?

A. I said I examined to-day, and I think I examined the same plans, many of them, two years ago, at Cochrane & Piquenard's office.

Q. Are these the same?

A. I should think they were. They have been making several changes in detail, one way or another, but the plans they represent to-day are the same plans they had two years ago, and the plans, I understand, adopted by the State.

Q. State, if you will, whether the building, so far as it has been erected, has been done in accordance with those plans and specifications.

A. I should think they hadn't—in fact, I know they haven't.

Q. State wherein there has been any deviation.

A. The plans don't show any form of construction in the shape of arches, piers, &c. in the basement, but they have a plan which has been drawn since, in which piers are laid out in part, but only a part of those show on the plan. We asked them as to those constructed in the building. They said they hadn't been drawn. Mr. Piquenard had sketched them at the building at the time, without making any definite plans for them.

Q. Have you made any estimate as to what that building will cost when completed under the plans and specifications upon which the work so far has proceeded?

A. I should judge, that the way they have modified the plans since they started, it would be next to impossible to get at the real cost. If the plans are allowed to be changed at every shift and corner, it becomes impossible to tell.

Q. Taking into consideration the amount of money already expended, and the amount of money that would be spent, what would be the probable cost, in your judgment?

A. I understand they have spent now about $900,000.

Q. Up to the 1st of December, $805,000.

A. Well, I don't know, sir. I looked at some drawings to-day, said to be made for the next story, the stone work, &c., and I looked at the design for the same thing, as adopted by the State—designs shown to me for the same plans—picked them out and pasted them together, and there is, I should judge, so far as the design for the next story, from 50 to 75 per cent. more than those shown on the plans as adopted. Taking that through in that way, if that method is to be carried on, you may swallow up from five to six million dollars, taking as a basis that story on which they now seem to be at work; those things are apt to grow and increase.

Q. I will ask you in regard to some of the arches: What is your opinion about them, as to whether the arches over the air ducts will stand or not?

A. They are very flat, sir—hardly think they would hold their weight.

Q. How long, and how wide are those arches?

A. Between six and seven feet.

Q. How long are they?

A. They run the whole length of the building north and south; from the north to the center—from the south to the center. They are very long. Of course there is no particular amount of weight on them.

Mr. BUNN, Commissioner—

No weight on them at all.

A. I should think the arches spring about four inches.

Mr. ROBINSON, Commissioner—

Five inches.

A. I didn't measure.

By MR. ROBERTS:

C. Is that sufficiently strong for an arch to be self-supporting?

A. I shouldn't have been willing to support that arch myself.

Mr. BEVERIDGE, Commissioner—

Been very easy matter to tell by taking out the supports.

A. A matter of surprise that they hadn't been taken out before.

By Mr. ROBERTS:

Q. I will get you to state if you have made any examination of the work to day, as you made an examination some time ago, and gave the result to this committee.

A. I did, sir.

Q. You may state what the condition of the work was.

A. There has been a good deal of exposition of the work since I was here, because there are a good many holes in the walls, which expose more than when I was here before. I find a portion of those holes cut through expose a very fine quality of work, and a portion of them exposed, what I supposed it would prove, a very inferior quality of work as compared with the other; that is, to day, you take on one side—the north side of the corridor—as compared with the other, there is no comparison; one is very inferior, the other very good indeed.

Q. State whether it is improved any since you examined it in the winter.

A. I don't think it has.

Q. State whether it is likely to grow better—to make a good job.

A. Don't think it will ever set.

Mr. Bunn, Commissioner—

Are you still of opinion that the walls would fall down?

A. I never said they would.

Mr. Bunn:

Q. You said they would crush out.

A. I think so now.

By Mr. Roberts:

Q. What is the rule with regard to good mortar?

A. It will harden and make a solid mass.

Mr. Beveridge, Commissioner—

Q. If that was a brick [illustrating with one of three specimens on the table] from the very softest part of the wall, and the mortar there became that hard, would the other part of the wall become as hard?

A. (Taking a specimen and examining.) There is something to be noticed there to a very large extent. There are pockets there now, which are nothing but clean sand, showing that the mortar was not properly mixed. That mortar, (pointing to specimen,) was good, it came out of the cement mortar, but there was a lack of mixing in those sand pockets very considerably.

Q. Well, if that mortar had been good, Mr. Boynton, at the time you saw it in the winter, ought the wall to improve from that time to this?

A. Yes, sir, become as hard as that mortar, (pointing to specimen) within the time, to a reasonable distance from the outside, and since I came to-day, some I have seen as hard as that.

Q. I understood you, when you were here before, that you were superintending the erection of a large building in Chicago, the walls of which had been exposed. I will ask what building that was?

A. That was the Pacific Hotel.

Q. State what effect the winter had on those walls—whether they presented the same appearance that these walls do now?

A. I have no information whether they have dried.

Q. That is a large building, is it? How thick are the walls?

A. Two feet four inches.

Mr. Robinson, Commissioner:

Q. How long have you known Mr. Starck?

A. Two years.

Q. What was he doing?

A. He was in Springfield.

Q. Has he any work about Chicago?

A. Don't think he has.

Q. You regard him as a good architect?

A. As far as I saw.

Q. How much opportunity have you had to judge of his capacity as an architect?

A. From inquiries that I have made.

Q. Who did you inquire of?

A. Mr. Piquenard says he is a good architect.

Q. Does he tell you so?

A. Yes, sir. He has worked for Mr. Piquenard. Of course he hasn't worked for me, and I havn't examined any building he has constructed.

Q. Do you know Mr. Sloan's character as a builder?

A. First class.

Q. A man of ability in his profession?

A. Yes, sir.

Q. Your statement is that some of this work over here is very good, and some very unfair. How is the work, Mr. Boynton, in the cellar or basement part?

A. The sub-cellar, I should think, is good work.

Q. A portion of the walls are good; did you examine the walls in the west side—the main corridor where there is a large hole cut through the wall?

A. That on the west side, some of it, is better, but it isn't good work.

Q. Do you say good or bad work?

A. Better than some.

Q. Good or bad, fair or how is it? I don't ask how it is as compared with the other.

A. I have seen fairer work and have seen worse—a great deal better there.

Q. How long have you been an architect—worked at the business?

A. I have been an architect some thirty-five years.

Q. How long have you lived in Chicago?

A. Eighteen years.

Q. Did you make a plan for this house—I don't remember—for this State House?

A. No, sir.

Q. You made a plan for the Iowa State House, for which Piquenard & Cochrane made a plan also. Whose plan was adopted?

A. Mine received the premium.

Q. Whose plan was adopted?

A. The last time I saw, the Governor hadn't adopted any plan.

Q. Yours received the premium?

A. Yes, sir.

Q. You and they had been competing?

A. There—yes, sir.

Q. What was it worth to do a job of brick work such as the best of that there?

A. Do you mean simply the work, or the material too?

Q. Yes, that's what I mean.

A. Well, I should judge that such work as that could have been laid last year, including the brick work and mortar, according to the specifications, and according to the standard of the best walls, for from twelve to thirteen dollars. I think I could have contracted for that.

By Mr. McMillan:

Q. You mean by the thousand?

A. Yes, sir.

By Mr. Roberts:

Q. That means measured in the wall?

A. Yes, in the wall.

By Mr. Robinson:

That's all.

By Mr. Roberts:

Q. You say the work is defective as to specifications?

A. Yes, sir, considering the specifications.

Q. Were you the architect on the penitentiary?

A. Yes, sir.

Q. Did you establish and make out the specifications, and measurements on that work which the State paid for?

A. I did.

—10

M. W. Carter, sworn, and examined by Mr. Roberts, as follows:

Q. What is your name.

A. M. W. Carter.

Q. Where do you reside?

A. In Chicago.

Q. What is your business?

A. I am a builder and contractor.

Q. How long have you been engaged in that business?

A. I have been engaged in the business for twenty-two or twenty-three years, sir.

Q. How long have you lived in Chicago?

A. About fifteen years.

Q. State whether or not you have examined the work upon the new State House.

A. Yes, sir; I have this day.

Q. State what the result of that examination has been. If you have examined the brick work, please state what the result of your examination has been.

A. Yes, sir; I examined the brick work more particularly than anything else. There is some very excellent brick work there, and some very poor.

Q. What is the difference?

A. The difference between the good and the bad is owing to the mortar—the defect is in the mortar.

Q. What is the reason of the defect in the mortar?

A. That might be difficult to tell, taking it as it is now. It is plain to be seen it is not right. Why it is not right is that the proper ingredients were not put together to make good mortar.

Q. Did you examine any of the lime and sand being used.

A. I saw some piles of sand there; I saw some river sand; looked to be river sand; the sand seemed to be pretty good quality; not entirely free from dirt; I saw a pile of yellow sand lying there that had a pretty large proportion of loam in it.

Q. Could good mortar be made from that kind of sand, in your judgment?

A. It could not be made as good, certainly, out of yellow loam sand.

Q. Do you know whether the mortar in those walls was made

of that yellow loam sand? Do you know whether that kind of sand was used there in making mortar?

A. No, sir; I can not tell after it is made. There are evidences there of improperly slackened lime in the mortar. There are pieces of white lime, about the size of a pea, in some portions of the wall which should not be there, and which does not occur in good mortar. In good mortar the lime and sand is so amalgamated that it is one body—one thing after being mixed. There are no different colors in it, or spots, or anything of the kind to it.

Q. Do you know anything about the kind of lime that was used there?

A. No, sir.

Q. Did you hear any of the contractors or architects say anything about what kind of lime was used?

By Mr. Robinson:

It is Lemont lime.

By Mr. Roberts:

Q. Do you know anything about the Lemont lime?

A. Very little. We don't see any of it in Chicago. Our firm never use it. I don't know anything about the lime.

Q. Do you know anything about the reputation of the Lemont lime? State what proportion of those walls, in your judgment, are good and what proportion are bad.

A. I could not tell you. I didn't examine it far enough to tell. Perhaps it would be rather difficult to tell where the dividing line was. I may be mistaken as regards the points of the compass, but I think it is upon the east side of the building that the walls are good. The walls upon that side as a general thing appear to be good. Some of them are well hardened up for the time they have been laid.

Q. What was the defect in the walls that are defective, and will they ever make walls?

A. As I said before, the defect is in the mortar. In my opinion, it never will be a good wall.

Q. Should any of the walls be taken down?

A. I should pronounce them wholly unfit for a building of that kind.

Q. About what proportion of the walls are unfit for a building of that kind?

A. I am not prepared to say.

Q. About how much did you examine that was unfit?

A. Several of them upon the west side of that is of the partition walls, a portion of the right corridor wall as you go in from the north.

Q. Did you notice the cross walls?

A. Yes, sir; all of them are in the same condition.

Q. What should be done with those walls?

A. I would take them down and rebuild them with proper mortar.

Q. Did you examine the outside walls just within the stone walls, backing up against the stone walls?

A. I don't recollect examining any in the west part. There was some pretty good ones in the east part, backing up against the stone.

Q. Do you know Mr. Bolin-Starck?

A. I never saw him until to-day.

Q. Do you know anything about the manner in which he measured that work.

A. He explained to us the manner in which he measured it.

Q. State, if you will, in your judgment, whether that was the proper manner in which to measure it.

A. You are assuming that I know nothing about the contract.

Q. Did you see the specifications?

A. I saw two different specifications. I understand the work was not done according to either of the specifications I saw, and I know it was not built from either. I understood from Mr. Piquenard. He told me they had more general specifications.

Q. Did you notice the specifications Bolin-Starck showed you?

A. I think he showed me, or I think those I saw came from him.

Q. Will you state whether these walls were measured by him in accordance with those specifications, or as liberal as those specifications.

A. The way he explained it to me, I think he followed the letter of the specification. He measured the wall according to the letter of the specifications. But there is one large arch about twenty feet span, and some hundred feet or more long, he measured from the spring of the arch, and consequently his quantity in that one item alone was some four hundred thousand brick larger than any engineer would measure it. [The witness here explained upon a plat the nature of the arch referred to, and proceeded.] He measured every one above the spring of the arch solid, whereas all this should have been deducted.

Q. What does that arch sustain ?

A. I do not know. I looked at it. I don't know what they are going to do with it.

Q. Do you know whether that was the arch intended to be iron, and girders, by the specifications ?

A. I understood all these arches were put in in place of the iron girders.

Q. Is the floor laid upon this arch ?

A. Yes, sir.

Q. It is the arch upon which the floor is laid that he measured, solid.

A. Yes, sir. Any engineer, in the absence of any direction, would not measure that solid.

Q. How much difference do you say it would make ?

A. I made a moderate calculation of it. If I didn't err, it would be about 400,000 brick.

Q. State if you know from what conversation you have had with him, what his capabilities are as an engineer for making that measurement.

A. He talked very intelligently about it, as a man understanding the business perfectly. From what I heard him say, I have no reasonable doubt that he measured it correctly.

Q. Is he, in your judgment, competent to measure that kind of work ?

A. From my slight acquaintance with him, I should say he was. My acquaintance with him is very limited.

Q. Does he seem to understand engineering and architecture ?

A. Yes, sir. He seems to understand mathematical calculations.

Q. Do you know anything about the manner in which the brick walls, abutting up against the stone walls, were measured ?

A. He said he got the best average of it he could. He could not tell just what it was, now.

Q. State whether that would be the proper way to measure it ?

A. To have done it correctly, the measurement should have been made at each successive course of stone, then you could see just how thick the stone was. Of course, after it is all laid up you can't tell exactly how thick the stone are, but you can approximate it.

Q. Have you examined the specifications upon which the State House is to be built and completed?

A. Only in a very rapid manner. Not carefully, with a view of giving an opinion upon that point.

Q. Have you made any calculation. Can you approximate anything near as to what the building will cost when completed, under the plan and specifications under which it is proposed to be built?

A. I can not. It would require the labor of a good many days to do that with any satisfaction, and the longer time spent upon it, the nearer you would get it correctly.

Q. State if you know anything about whether the work, so far as it has been done, is done according to the original plans and specifications?

A. I know the brick work is not done according to the specifications I have read.

Q. Wherein does it differ?

A. In the mortar, sir.

Q. State what the difference is between the specifications and the mortar there in the walls?

A. It is simply this: that if the mortar put in the walls had been according to the specifications, it would have set. It is not set, and therefore, was not according to the specifications.

Q. Will it ever set?

A. I don't believe it will. That is a matter of opinion, only.

Q. Will that ever become a first class job, in your opinion?

A. It never will. That is my opinion, decidedly.

Q. What would be the proper course to pursue now with those walls?

A. Tear them down by all means.

Q. Would it be safe to erect so heavy and large a building as that upon those walls?

A. It would not.

Examination by Mr. Robinson, on behalf the State House Commissioners:

Q. You do not give your opinion as to what proportion of the walls are good and what bad?

A. No, sir.

Q. How long were you there examining them?

A. About two or three hours.

Q. Would it not, in that space of time, necessarily be a very imperfect examination?

A. Not in regard to the quality of the work. We were there long enough to discover that. Of course, if a man were to go over and pass upon every wall separately, it would require more time.

Q. You say there are good and bad walls there?

A. Yes, sir.

Q. You didn't notice the walls backing up against the stone. You didn't notice any bad work in that?

A. No, sir; I don't know that I did.

Q. Was it the cross walls you noticed?

A. Yes, sir; the interior walls.

Q. What is the quality of that brick for strength and durability—the brick that has been laid up there?

A. It is good, fair brick. Its power of resistance of pressure is not so great as some of our Chicago or Milwaukee brick.

Q. Is resistance to pressure an important quality in brick?

A. Yes, sir.

Q. When a wall is perfectly level, does brick in the wall ever crush?

A. Yes, sir.

Q. How many pounds of weight can you put upon the bottom brick in a wall that is sixty feet high—how many pounds to the square inch; supposing the wall to be perfectly level, could you get weight enough to crush a brick?

A. You have asked two questions.

Q. Have you ever made a calculation in your life how much weight there was upon a brick in a wall?

A. Yes sir, I can make it here in a short time.

Q. Take a stone a foot square—a cubic foot of stone—then saw it up into inch square blocks or cubes, how high will they go?

A. There would be 144 if I understand the question.

Q. What would that solid foot of stone weigh originally?

A. That depends upon the stone—kind of stone.

Q. Say the Lemont?

A. It would be about 160 pounds.

Q. Would that weight crush your thumb even?

A. I would not like to have my thumb under it.

Q. How much pressure will a brick stand to the square inch?

A. I am not prepared to answer that question.

Q. Would it not stand ten times as much as a wall forty-four feet high?

A. I should think it would.

Q. Would it not stand all the crushing power you could put on it if the wall was plumb?

A. Very likely.

Q. You say part of those walls are very fine.

A. Yes sir, first rate quality.

Q. Do you know what kind of lime and sand had been used in those good walls, so as to tell what quality it was?

A. That is something that can not be told without analyzing it. You can see by the way the mortar is set, that is good; there is the appearance that some of the lime was not as well slacked as it should have been.

Q. What was it worth per thousand to put brick in the wall last year—you furnish the brick, the labor and all the materials measured in the wall?

A. I think our proposition for that work was about fourteen dollars per thousand.

Q. Was it not $17 50?

A. I don't think it was.

Q. If it were shown that it was $17 50 you would acknowledge you were mistaken, would you not?

A. Yes sir.

Q. Mr. Beveridge says it was exactly $17?

A. I am not in a proper condition to deny it.

Q. Do you think $14 was a fair price for it?

A. I am answering the question at random; that was doubtless made up from statistics which I had at the time, which I have not now. I don't remember what the price of brick was. If they have my written proposition I would rather take that than any estimate I would form now.

Q. Suppose this contract was let at the time you made that bid —this contract under which this work is done—would you say those walls were worth $14 per thousand ?

A. Yes sir.

Q. Suppose Mr. Clark (the man who put up the walls) and this man who measured them (Bolin-Starck), should come forward, and Clark who measured every wall as they went up: the thickness, hight and all, and give their measurements—which man would you rely upon the most ?

A. In the face of such a large discrepancy I should have the thing just measured right up. It can all be arrived at, within a hundred brick, with the exception of the outside wall; there might be a liberal allowance there.

Q. If Clark would come forward with his books and show the measurement of every wall, as it went up, and this other man would come forward with what he showed you this morning, which would you rely upon the most ?

A. One of the gentlemen I never saw in my life, and my acquaintance with the other is limited. I should have to have something to base my opinion upon, and I have not got it.

Q. Which man would have the best opportunity of being correct—the man that put the walls up and made the figures and kept them every day, or the other man ?

A. With regard to the outside walls: the man that put them up. In the other walls there would be no difference; it can be measured now as well as at any time.

Q. You simply base your judgment upon what Bolin-Starck told you. You saw none of his figures ?

A. That is true.

Q. Suppose it turns out that he has no qualifications, and is a rogue generally, what would be your opinion then ?

A. I would not think anything of him—I would not take his statements.

Re-examination by Mr. Roberts:

Q. I will ask you, if you measure these outside walls, solid brick and stone, then deduct the number of cubic feet of stone, would not that give the number of brick ?

A. Yes sir, of course.

By Mr. Beveridge :

Q. You would have to make some allowance for the projections upon the outside?

A. Yes sir.

Examination by Mr. Bobinson, continued :

(Some specimens of mortar attached to broken pieces of brick, taken from the walls of the State House, shown.)

Q. Give your opinion whether that is good mortar or not?

A. That seems to be very good mortar. There appears to be a little dry sand in there.

Q. How long, ordinarily, does it take mortar to get hard and set in walls of that thickness?

A. Mortar ought to set in at the rate of an inch per month, until you get up to a wall that is two feet thick. I don't think, however, that would be as hard in two years as it would eventually become, because I have observed that the oldest walls are the hardest.

Examination by Mr. McMillan, on behalf of the Commissioners :

Q. I understand that a contractor, doing brick work, can't do so much work—that is, his hands can't do so much work—in a given length of time, using bad mortar, as they can if they use good, rich mortar.

A. That is true.

Q. Then I would ask you this question. What inducement is there, to a contractor, to use bad mortar? Is there any pecuniary inducement?

A. There might be a mortar made out of certain kinds of lime and sand, that would work very well; a man could do an ordinary day's work with it, and it might have the appearance of being pretty good mortar, and afterwards disappoint expectations with regard to it. Using quick-lime and good, clean, sharp sand, there is no inducement at all to put in an extra quantity of sand, because all that is saved in the lime is lost in the labor.

Examination by Mr. Robinson, continued :

Q. Do you know Barnard as a contractor?

A. I have met him.

Q. Do you know what his character is as a contractor?

A. My impression of him is favorable. I have met him only a few times.

SANFORD LORING sworn, and examined by MR. ROBERTS, as follows:

Q. Where do you reside.

A. In Chicago.

Q. What is your business?

A. That of an architect.

Q. How long have you been engaged in that business?

A. It is about fifteen years since I first worked in an architect's office.

Q. Have you examined the work upon this new State House?

A. I called there this morning, early, and walked over the building.

Q. Did you make any examination of the work?

A. Yes, sir.

Q. State what that examination was, and the result of it.

A. My attention was called to the character of the brick work, and more particularly to the character of the mortar. I found a great deal of good work there, and a great deal that I call bad work. I found in the west part of the building there, the walls, or the mortar in the walls, was rather inferior. On the other part of the building it appeared to be very good, indeed. The brick work and mortar in the basement is excellent.

Q. What is the cause of the defect in the walls you found defective?

A. I don't know that I could give the cause; I would not attempt to do that; I only know the work. I should not accept such work in Chicago, because there is no occasion there for ever having that kind of work. The material is of such a character that I never discovered anything of the kind there.

By Mr. BEVERIDGE:

Q. Buildings never fall down in Chicago, do they?

A. Oh! yes, such things have happened, but not because we didn't have good mortar.

By Mr. ROBERTS:

Q. What was the cause of the Court House falling down?

A. The Court House didn't fall; it was the iron work—the roof; there was too much roof and too much snow.

Q. What was the cause of that mortar being bad?

A. I don't know, sir; I only know it is what I call bad mortar.

Q. Did you examine the lime and sand of which that mortar was made?

A. I examined some sand there that I was told was used in the building; there was some lime there which I should hope was not used. I didn't see any good lime about the premises; I saw a large pile of lime there which I took to be rubbish; it was in the basement; I didn't see any other there.

Mr. Robinson stated that the lime referred to was waste lime, that had been slacked and hardened, and could not be used.

Q. State what you saw of sand there.

A. I saw the two piles of sand; one seemed as though it had been washed; it was clean sand; it was as clean sand as I would expect to see. There was another pile of sand there that I would call loam sand; we do not allow people to use that kind of sand if we can help it.

Q. Is that loam sand good.

A. I would not allow it to be used in a building of mine. If the sand was used with cement, as I judge it has been, from the appearance of the wall below, it would make good mortar; but I never saw any good mortar made from that kind of sand used with quick lime.

Q. What proportion of those walls do you consider good, and what proportion bad.

A. That is difficult to tell, because I didn't examine with a view of finding that out. When I went there this morning I hardly knew what I went for, except as my attention was called to this thing and that thing about the building.

(Specifications attached to contract shown.)

Q. Examine those specifications and state how that work corresponds with the specifications.

A. I see it says, all brick wall above, to be laid with mortar composed of one part of cement, one part of lime slacked at least one week before using, and five parts of clean, sharp sand. I should judge a portion of that work was not laid up according to that specification. It says, "all inside cellar brick walls, to the hight of the present outside walls, will be laid with mortar composed of one part of cement and three parts of clean, sharp sand." There is a very marked difference between the mortar in the walls and that called for by that specification. There is not much differcnce between the kinds of mortar called for in these two specifications.

Q. State whether, in your judgment, if they had used the in gredients provided in the specifications, of good quality, in the proportions stated, it would have made good work.

A. Yes, sir, I should expect it to make good mortar.

Q. State if the mortar in which those walls above the cellar was made in accordance with those specifications?

A. I should say not; a portion of it.

Q. What proportion has been laid in accordance with the specifications, and what proportion has not been?

A. I could not state, as I did not examine it carefully enough; I saw a large quantity of the work in the west portion of the building, of which I should say the mortar was not made according to the specifications; that upon the east side—I should say there has been cement used there.

Q. Will that which you examined ever make a first class job?

A. I would rather answer that question ten years hence.

Q Give your judgment.

A. I should very much prefer to have a different class of work. I should not expect to see it improve very much in time, but having had no experience with that class of work I can not say whether it will grow harder or not.

Q. Would it be a first class job of work if it was as good as the east wall.

A. Yes, sir.

Q. State whether, in your judgment, it is proper to erect so large and so expensive a building, upon walls such as they are?

A. I should prefer to leave the walls as they are upon the east side. I would prefer to take them down and relay them. It would depend upon what is going to be done above. I was there this morning and just passed over the work, and a person who would pretend to pass judgment after inspecting those walls but a few hours, would do what I would not do.

Q. Have you examined the general plans by which this State House is to be built?

A. Yes, sir.

Q. Can you approximate the cost of the State House after it is finished according to the plans and specifications?

A. I could give a run and jump at it. There has been expended some $820,000, as I understand it. I could not say. I can say this, however, from my experience as an architect, that they will expend all the money you will give them. That is about as definite as it can be put. I found from the few questions I asked in the office, that they had no definite idea what they were going to use, only in parts of the work; and until somebody knows just what is going to be done, etc., nobody can tell what it will cost. I talked with Mr. Piquenard, and others in the office then, about it. I asked what is this or that to be made of. One would say it is to be made of iron. Then I would ask another the same question, and he would say it was to be made of stone. "It is to be made of cut stone, if we can have money enough," would be the answer. In that rambling state no one can tell how much money will be expended. I can have the building finished up on those plans and expend all the money you will give me. And yet, I can carry out the general plans given them, (I have not examined the specifications carefully,) but so far as the general plans are concerned I can carry them out, and erect the building within the limits fixed by the Constitution.

Q. What will be the cost, in your judgment, of the building, if carried out in the way they have been going on, using the materials they have used so far?

A. There would be no difference in the appearance of the external finish how the internal portions were made, whether you make the door cases of wood, stone or marble, yet there would be a good deal of difference in the cost.

Q. Do those specifications provide what sort of finish it shall be?

A I don't know. I did n't examine them. If I were going to erect a building I would inform the architects how much room I wanted, and tell them how much money I had to expend. Then let the plans be made and details all filled out, then let the contract be signed with reliable parties, then I would expect to know what my building would cost. I noticed they were revising the plans this morning. They did n't know just what they would use themselves.

Q. Just state, if you can, from the examination you made of the plans you saw, what that building will cost. Give your judgment of the approximate cost of the building when completed.

A. My estimate would be of no value to you at all.

Q. You think it can be built for the amount to which they are limited ?

A. Yes, sir, but you can spend three times that amount of money.

Q. Did you meet Mr. Bolin-Starck over there to day ?

A. No, sir, I did not see him there. I met him away from the building.

Q. Did you have any conversation with him about the measurement of those walls. Did he explain to you the manner in which he measured the work ?

A. Yes sir, he stated to me the way he measured it. He measured it according to the specifications.

Q. State whether he was liberal in his measurements or not, if he measured it the way he told you.

A. You cannot be liberal; you have to confine yourself to the specifications. There was one point, however, I should have stretched the specifications in. My attention was called to a very large arch in the cellar, and then my attention was called to the specification with reference to the measurement of arching. I was informed by Mr. Bolin-Starck that he measured that arch solid, that he had simply taken out what would be the spandrel of the arch. That he had deducted that because it was filled with con crete, and that it had been measured up and paid for separately. But he measured the whole solid from the spring of the arch, and in that hole you can put 300,000 brick, or, I guess, 400,000 if you try. That I consider very liberal measurement. I think I should have asked some questions before making that allowance.

Q. What is your judgment as to his competency to make such a measurement, from your conversation with him.

A. He seemed to be intelligent and sufficiently familiar with such thing to measure the work.

Examinatiin by Mr. Robinson, *on behalf of the Commissioners*:

Q. You say part of the work is very good, and some bad ?

A. Yes, sir.

Q. But the proportion you are not able give.

A. No, sir.

Q. But upon that portion which is bad you would rather risk

your judgment ten years from now; you mean by that it will harden and get better ?

A. It may.

[Specimens of mortar attached to pieces of bricks shown.]

Q. Examine that mortar and see if that is good mortar. [Witnees examines the mortar.]

A. Yes sir, that appears to be good mortar.

Q. Speaking of the brick itself, separate from the mortar, are they a good quality of brick ?

A. Yes, sir, they seem to be very good brick.

Q. You say the brick work in the basement is very good ?

A. Yes, sir, I examined some that was very good.

Q. There was some portion of the west walls that did not appear to be good work ?

A. Yes, sir.

Q. But the proportion you are not able to give ?

A. No, sir.

Q. Do you know about what it was worth last year to lay those brick in the wall, finding the lime, sound brick, and all the materials, and put in the wall ?

A. I don't know what your prices are here for men, sand, etc.

Q. What was it in Chicago last year, say in the fall ?

A. They ranged about at $13 00. I believe that would be a fair average laid up in the wall.

Q. Did you examine the brick work upon the west side of the building sufficiently to tell whether there was any cement in it ?

A. I should say there was no cement in it at all. I examined it very carefully, because I was surprised to find it as it was.

Q. Is there any cement used in that mortar ? [Referring to brick lying upon the table.]

A. That is what I would call, in Chicago, good lime mortar. That is a good deal better than that in the west wall.

Q. Did you examine that large hole upon the west side that has been cut through one of the cross walls ?

A. Yes, sir.

Q. How was that work then ? Good or bad ?

A. My recollection is, that it seemed to be better than in other parts.

Q. What manner of examination did you give ? Did you go upon the top of the walls, or did you just stand up beside the walls?

A. I went upon the top and examined it from the side also. I cut into it with my knife.

Q. Is there any better way to examine them than to cut into the walls?

A. No, sir; that is as good a way to do it as any.

Q. You stated that your judgment would not be worth anything as to the amount it would take to complete the building.

A. I could give a judgment, but it would only be my idea. The only way you could get an intelligent answer to that question would be, to look at the complete specifications, and know just what was to go into the building. No one can give an intelligent idea until the plans are completed and parties are prepared to do the work. If the plans are made out complete—all the details and specifications—a man can have a pretty good judgment as to the cost. If a man knows just what he wants he should be able to decide the cost to a cent.

Q. Do you know Barnard, Carter and Decker as architects and builders?

A. Yes, sir.

Q. What is their reputation?

A. Their reputations are good; as good as we have in Chicago.

Q. Suppose those men made complete plans and specifications, figuring as to the cost of a building, would you have any faith in them?

A. I would have confidence in them, but I would rather have contractors do the figuring, because architects have not the requisite intelligence upon it to make estimates.

By Mr. McMillan:

Q. Do you know whether that sand was washed before it was used?

A. I should think it was used in the wall without being washed.

MONDAY, *May* 29, 1871.

GEORGE O. GARNSEY, sworn.

Direct Examination—By Mr. ROBERTS.

Q. What is your name, residence and business?

A. George O. Garnsey: I live in Chicago, and am an architect.

Q. How long have you been in this business?

A. Fourteen years.

Q. Do you know the architects of the new State House, Piquenard and Cochrane?

A. Yes, sir.

Q. How long have you known them?

A. Mr. Piquenard a year, not intimately; have known Mr. Cochrane four or five years.

Q. Have you examined the walls of the new State House?

A. I have.

Q. You may just state what sort of a job you consider the brick work in those walls?

A. Well, sir, some of it I find very good; in the sub-basement I find the brick work a very good job.

Q. That means the cellar?

A. Yes, sir; almost all the brick work in the west wing, in the basement of the building, I should pronounce not first-class work.

Q. Just state wherein it is defective.

A. I consider the brick very good, but the material isn't.

Q Wherein is the material defective?

A. I think the sand and lime not good.

Q. Did you examine the sand there?

A. Yes, sir.

Q. State what kind.

A. I shouldn't call it first-class sand; too much loam in it.

Q. Is it possible to make a good job out of that sand?

A. I think not, sir.

Q. Do you know anything about the kind of lime used?

A. No, sir.

Q. Do you know anything about the Lemont lime?

A. No, sir--I would qualify that statement—I haven't seen it worked with this sand, and therefore know nothing about it.

Q. What is the character of Lemont lime?

A. It hasn't a first-class reputation.

Q. What do you say of the mortar of those walls in the basement?

A. Not according to the specifications; not what I should expect if it was on my work.

Q. You have examined other parts of the building?

A. Yes, sir.

Q. What portion of the walls do you consider bad?

A. Those in the west wing, the interior walls of the west wing and part of the outside walls.

Q. What proportion will that make of the whole walls of the basement?

A. I think perhaps a quarter; I can show you by the diagram.

Q. Did you make a diagram?

A. Yes, sir; I made this copy from the plan of the basement, and then on that made a diagram of each wall of the building. (The witness here exhibits his diagram, explaining various parts of it.) It is a diagram of all the walls of the basement; it was made in Mr. Starck's office; I went to the building and measured with a tape-line, and then estimated from these diagrams.

Q. Did you estimate what proportion was bad?

A. Yes, sir; I will show you in this plan of the building; (witness here exhibits another paper,) this, you understand, is a tracing from the plan given to me by the Commissioners.

Q. Just state whether, in your judgment, those walls are sufficient for the building proposed to be erected on them?

A. Do you mean in quality? No, sir, they are not.

Q. State whether, in your judgment, it is justifiable to erect that kind of a building on those walls?

A. No, sir.

Q. What ought to be done?

A. Take them down and rebuild.

Q. Have you examined the specifications, to see whether the brick work was done in accordance with them?

A. It is not.

Q. Wherein does it differ?

A. The specifications call for first-class work in every particular; it isn't first-class work.

Q. Have you estimated the number of brick in those walls?

A. I have.

Q. State your means of estimating and what your result was.

A. Mr. Starck was the surveyor and architect; I requested him to assist me in making the diagram; the diagram is made from measurement taken on the building, and from the basement plan which I have made tracing of; and then I went to the building and put my own measurement on the diagram, and figured the quantity of brick from the diagram.

Q. What number did you make it?

A. (Taking out a book), six millions three hundred and eighty-seven thousand seven hundred and fifteen.

Q. State whether or not a full measurement?

A. I made a liberal measurement.

Q. Did you examine those arches in the sub-basement? If you did, state how they were measured; how the bricks in those arches in the sub-basement in the cellar were measured?

A. There are two sorts of arches.

Q. I mean those long arches.

A. One is the arches supporting the floors; I measured them solid from the spring of the arch.

Q. Is that the customary way of measuring that kind of arch?

A. I hardly think it is; the usual way is to strike a line from the spring to the center. The reason why I measured in this way was to give a liberal measurement; I understood it was the contract that that kind of measurement should be made.

Q. Have you, at any time, examined the work on the State House? and if so, when—before this time?

A. Two years ago.

Q. What work did you examine then.

A. The foundations up to the grade level; up to where the Joliet stone now starts.

Q. Including the whole sub-basement?

A. Yes, sir; the sub basement was not entirely finished.

Q. Was it done in accordance with the specifications?

A. I don't consider it was; the specifications required the joints in the stone work to be a quarter of an inch, nothing more nor less. I measured, at that time, joints from a quarter of an inch up to three inches and a half.

Q. What difference does that make in the cost of the work?

A. It entirely did away with a certain amount of setting that would have been done, to bring down to a close fitting joint—they were laid without bush hammering.

Q. Did the specifications call for bush hammering?

A. They did; that is the only way to bring the stone down to the surface. I estimated the difference in labor saved in the joints to the contractors, at $37,500—the entire work upon the foundation at that period.

Q. I will ask you if, in the examination, there was more stone work in the foundation than necessary?

A. I measured, Saturday, one wall six feet three inches on the top, built to support a wall three feet two inches—I would say nine feet three inches, instead of six feet three inches—to support a wall three feet two inches, running the whole length of the building.

Q. Was that necessary?

A. It was not.

Q Have you examined the size of the stone in the basement?

A. I did.

Q. Were they in accordance with the specifications?

A. No, sir; the specifications stipulated a certain size; nothing more, nothing less. I counted twenty-nine stones that varied from the specifications.

Q. What difference in the cost did you estimáte the variation to amount to?

A. $96,000.

Q. Have you examined the specifications with regard to the size of the stone in the basement?

A. No, sir.

Q. In regard to these large joints—would it make any difference in the bids for a contract, whether the joints were large or small?

A. I estimated the difference at $37,500.

Q. You could take it at that much less?

A. Yes, sir; there could have been saved $37,500 if the specifications had been three and one-half inches instead of a quarter inch joint.

Q. You may state if you know anything about the original estimate of the cost of the foundation?

A. Mr. Cochrane, when he was my partner, made an estimate of the foundation. I cannot state the amount of that estimate.

Q. Do you know what it cost?

A. I figured the cost of the excess over Mr. Cochrane's estimate at $211,751.

Q. Do you know what sort of stone was used in the foundation?

A. No, sir.

Q. Do you know whether it was Joliet stone or not?

A. No, sir, not Joliet stone.

Q. Do you know what would be the relative cost between that and the other stone, or whether there is any difference or not?

Q. Mr. Robinson, Commissioner:

We can show you the bids. We have all the bids from the Lemont quarry and the other quarry, and we can give you the original bids.

Mr. Roberts:

That will do.

Q. You may state if you examined the foundation for the dome, and the balance of the building?

A. Yes, sir.

Q. For the dome—how built?

A. On the rock, on concrete, with a rock foundation.

Q. For the balance of the building?

A. On the soil.

Q. What effect, if any, would that have when the weight of the superstructure comes upon the foundation—part being upon solid rock foundation, and part upon the soil?

A. The settlement, I should say, would be very uneven. The balance of the building would, in my judgment, settle away from the dome.

Q. What would be the reason?

A. Because the dome, being upon the rock, the settlement would be less, while the superstructure, being built upon the soil, would settle more or less for two or three years. I should consider that a very faulty construction.

Q. Have you ever estimated what this buildihg would cost when completed?

A. I have made no detailed estimate. I have my idea.

Q. What, in your judgment, will be the cost, at the rate it has cost already?

A. I don't think it could be finished for less than $5,000,000—that was my original idea when we designed the building.

Q. Who drew up those designs?

A. I did, sir.

Q. Were you in partnership with Mr. Cochrane?

A. I was.

Q. About this concrete work—describe what it was, whether good or not.

A. I know nothing about the concrete below the wall, but the concrete on the arches of the basement, I shouldn't say, was good work. Concrete ought to be as hard as rock—and I guess you could punch a stick down six inches into it easy enough.

Q. How long has that been so?

A. Couldn't say.

Q. Well, now, in regard to the building of this brick and stone work—were there any iron anchors, anchoring the brick to the stone?

A. I was informed there were none.

Q. State whether they were necessary, in your judgment, or not?

A. I have never seen a building built without them before.

Q. Explain the necessity for them.

A. The stone work needs to be fastened up with the brick work, and there is no way to tie the brick to the stone work except by iron anchors anchored into the stone work with a little "Y" bar that there may be no settlement in the brick work away from the stone work; otherwise the inside will settle away from the stone work. The weight of the floors is going to stretch it more or less; and now when that work there settles, the brick must settle away, and the iron anchor not being there they must crack right apart when the weight comes upon them.

Q. You were a partner of Mr. Cochrane's at the time these plans were adopted?

A. Yes, sir, I was—I drew the plans.

Q. What was the firm—Cochrane & Garnsey?

A. Yes, sir.

Q. How much did they get?

A. The firm received $3,000—premium—money paid to the firm.

Q. That was paid as premium?

A. Yes, sir.

Mr. Robinson, Commissioner:

Mr. Garnsey has sworn to all that two years ago—it is all in that report.

Mr. ROBERTS:

I have been requested to ask these questions. I never read that report.

Q. You may state whether the premium was paid over to Mr. Cochrane.

A. Mr. Cochrane came to Springfield and received the premium—$3,000—to my knowledge, afterwards.

Q. Do you know whether there was any money paid, by Mr. Cochrane, for the purpose of getting his plan adopted?

A. Yes, sir.

Q. If so, state——

Mr. ROBINSON, Commissioner:

Yes, sir? Hold on! You say you know; but, sir, you don't know. I have heard him swear before.

Mr. ROBERTS;

I suppose what Mr. Cochrane told him as to how he got it——

Mr. ROBINSON, Commissioner:

I suppose not; he swears to what Mr. Cochrane told him.

Mr. ROBERTS:

Q. State what you know about it.

A. The firm books show $2,700, and some odd dollars, paid out by Mr. Cochrane, and he returned it to the firm as paid to get the plans adopted—the books of Cochrane & Garnsey. He came back from Springfield with $300, and said he had paid the rest to different parties to get the plans adopted. I say $300—about $300.

Q. Have those plans been changed in any respect—if so, in what?

A. The arrangement has been changed considerably. The dome has been enlarged, the sub-basement has been added which the original plan didn't call for.

Q. Would the changes affect the cost of the buildings—if so, about how much?

A. I haven't estimated. I shouldn't like to make a statement without estimating, but if the plans be carried out, as stated, I should say the building would cost about $5,000,000—which would make it $1,500,000 more than was intended.

Q. Do you remember what the original estimate was?

A. I think two million and about seven hundred thousand—I can't swear positively.

Cross-Examination, *by* MR. ROBINSON, *Commissioner:*

Q. Mr. Garnsey, you say that the wall ought to be anchored to the stone wall?

A. That is my judgment.

Q. Describe, so that the Committee can hear you, in what manner the walls ought to be anchored together.

A. By iron anchors.

Q. How large?

A. That depends on the place in the building. Place them wherever the spaces call for them, and about sixteen inches apart.

Q. How far apart would you leave them?

A. In a blank wall, three feet apart.

Q. How large would you have them?

A. I couldn't tell you exactly how large—the part of the work would altogether determine that.

Q. You have seen the walls; how large would you have them —those bars of iron—if you had been building?

A. That isn't for you to ask.

Q. But you can answer, I say, in your judgment?

A. The length I couldn't give you, because the cut stone runs into the wall, two feet in some places, in others a foot; that would make the anchors of different length; as to the size of the iron, you use them from an inch and three quarters to two inches.

Q. How far would you let them run into the brick?

A. The locality would determine that.

Q. You say the brick wall would settle away from the stone wall but for the anchors?

A. I think the sag of the beams would draw the brick wall away from the stone work.

Q. When you talk about the settling, which do you mean, the brick from the stone, or the stone from the brick?

A. Both ways.

Q. Do you say the anchor will hold them up?

A. Yes sir.

Q. That is if they don't break?

A. Wrought iron anchors put in that way would not break.

Q. You spoke of your examination two years ago; you spoke of finding joints three inches and a half apart. Did you find them pretty generally about that size?

—12

A. Yes sir; they ran from a quarter inch to three and a half.

Q. What proportion were three and a half?

A. Couldn't answer.

Q. Your judgment?

A. No judgment about it, for two years have elapsed since I saw them.

Q. You can state your judgment—those covered up now?

A. Yes sir.

Q. I thought so. Do you think any of them not covered up were three and a half inches?

A. Couldn't tell, sir.

Q. Are there none in the side walls?

A. Couldn't tell, sir.

Q. Was it a frequent thing, or an occasional only?

A. A frequent thing.

Q. Was it a horizontal or a perpendicular joint where you found these?

A. On the top of the wall, where I saw them, I 'spose would be horizontal.

Q. Where was it?

A. All over the building, in different parts.

Q. When was it you stuck a stick down six inches into the concrete?

A. I didn't do it.

Q. Did you see anybody do it?

A. Yes sir, I did.

Q. To-day?

A. Saturday.

Q. Whereabouts?

A. Couldn't tell you till I took you there.

Q. Can't you explain so that these gentlemen can understand?

A. I was on the building three hours—I couldn't tell exactly. I think it was in the west wing.

Q. To the southwest or northwest?

A. Couldn't say.

Q. Did you leave the stick there?

A. Couldn't tell.

Q. Did you leave the hole there?

A. Couldn't tell, I didn't take it away with me.

Q. Who was with you?

A. No one.

Q. I judge not—when did you go down to see the building?

A. Saturday morning.

Q How much time since then, sir, have you been on the work?

A. Pretty much all the time.

Q. How long?

A. I went up Saturday morning, first thing, and staid some time, about an hour and a half.

Q. How much time since?

A. Well, there have been two days since.

Q. How long were you there Saturday?

A. An hour and a half—first part of the morning.

Q. How long at other times?

A. Couldn't tell.

Q. Your judgment is all I ask.

A. I was there all day Sunday—not all day—I was there off and on. I might say all day. I was there three hours and a half at one time—couldn't say how many times afterwards.

Q. That is all the time you have had to do this measurement?

A. Yes sir; all the time I have been on the building.

Q. Have you put the tape lines on the walls yourself, and made the calculation yourself?

A. Yes sir, I have.

Q. Entirely?

A. Yes sir.

Q. Describe how you got at the measurement.

A. I had Mr. Starck assist me in making these diagrams; in fact I made out the diagrams from the plan; then he went with me to the building, and with Gen. Turchin; then I put the tape line on the walls and measured it, and put it on the diagrams, perhaps not on all; then I counted the number of the brick in the walls, measured the openings and put that on; then I took the diagrams of the tracing and went to Mr. Starck's office and figured till one o'clock last night.

Q. That's all the chance you have had to make these measurements?

A. That is all I desired.

Q. Tell the committee how you got at the measurement of those arches in the basement?

A. Went in and measured them.

Q. Just describe how you measured them.

A. With a rule and tape line.

Q. You measured from the spring to the top?

A. To the apex.

Q. That means the top, don't it?

A. It does sometimes.

Q. I thought so; I never knew an apex that wasn't at the top.

A. I have.

Q. Well, from the spring of the arch you say; and how could you tell how thick it was up to the apex, as you will have it?

A. The arch underneath has the entire floor to support.

Q. How did you get at the thickness of the floor?

A. I saw the thickness of the floor where you come into the corridors; that's the only way I could get at it.

Q. Floors all the same thickness?

A. No sir; I think not; the floor under the dome I figured of entirely different thickness; I got that from Mr. Clark.

Q. Did Mr. Clark have his books by to show you?

A. No, sir, he just told us.

Q. So you relied on him for that?

A. Yes sir.

Q. There is an arch underneath in each of those rooms?

A. I estimated the floor, except the dome, all the same thickness—I knew they must be.

Q. Is the level of the arches all the same in the sub-basements?

A. The crown of the arch is the same hight from the floor.

Q. Your recollection is they are all the same thickness?

A. Eight inches.

Q. All eight inches except the dome?

A. Yes sir.

Q. Do you recollect about the dome?

A. Sixteen inches.

Q. You said something about an excess of cost of ninety-six thousand dollars?

A. That was the estimate I made on the size of the stone (looking at his memorandum), as differing from the specification in the foundation—$96,000.

Q. Did the stone cost that much more than the work—you mean if it had been made according to the specifications it would have been that much less?

A. Yes sir.

Q. Do you regard that as a good foundation up to the base line?

A. Yes sir.

Q. You spoke awhile ago about your tying together the brick work with bars of iron?

A. Yes sir; tie the brick work to the stone work.

Q. You were a partner of Mr. Cochrane's at the time those plans were made out and submitted?

A. The original design; yes sir.

Q. You say there was an estimate as to what the building would cost—what was it? $2,700,000, didn't you say?

A. Yes sir.

Q. You were a partner—did you tell the Commissioners that would be the cost of the building?

A. No, sir; my partner did—so I understood—I wasn't there.

Q. Did you believe they were correct estimates?

A. I didn't make the estimates—I believe nothing about it, for I knew nothing about it; Mr. Cochrane made the estimate and put his own name to it.

Q. Didn't you say you believed at the time it would cost $5,000,000?

A. No, Mr. Robinson.

Q. You did.

A. What I meant to say was, what the building would cost now —I didn't mean to say that was the original estimate.

Q. I recollect there was the same trouble before with your testimony; you were then a partner with Mr. Cochrane?

A. Our partnership has been dissolved.

Q. Didn't you and he have a good deal of difficulty?

A. I think he swindled me a little.

Q. Did you and he have a good deal of ill-feeling?

A. I have just the feeling towards him I have towards the man that robs me.

Q. You are an enemy to him?

A. I have got over all that; two years have passed.

Q. You were down here, and testified two years ago?

A. Yes, sir; about that time.

Q. You testified the books would show about $2,700 paid for getting the plans adopted ?

A. Yes, sir.

Q. Do you recollect what Cochrane said—to whom he paid it ?

A. Commissioners and other parties.

Q You didn't swear that then ?

A. I swear it now ; he told me so.

Q. Don't you remember you said, in your former testimony, he paid Beckwith $1,000, for the purpose of controlling me ?

A. I said that at the time. Yes, sir.

Q. Now you say that Cochrane paid it to the Commissioners ?

A. Yes, sir ; $2,700.

Q. You said he paid $1,000 to get Beckwith to buy me.

A. I said so, two years ago.

Q. Did you say what he had done with the balance of the money before ?

A. He paid it to the Commissioners and others.

Q. Did he tell you generally Commissioners ?

A. He wouldn't tell me who.

Q. Did he say he had bought them all ?

A. He didn't tell me. I thought it was a cheap buy.

Q. Didn't you state he paid Beckwith $1,000 ?

A. Our books show that.

Q That would leave $1,700 outside ; did you swear two years ago he had bought the Commissioners ?

A. I think I did.

Q. Where are those books now ? In possession of Mr. Cochrane ?

A. Yes, sir.

Q. Are they in your control now ?

A. I have not seen them for some years ; Mr. Cochrane took charge of them.

Anthony Eitner sworn and examined by Mr. Robinson, on behalf of the Commissioners.

Q. Where do you reside ?

A. In St. Louis.

Q. What is your business ?

A. Brick mason.

Q. How long have you worked at the business?

A. About sixteen or seventeen years.

Q. You may state to the committee whether or not you have done a large amount of work, or how large experience or small; give them some idea of your experience in building.

A. I have carried on business in St. Louis for twelve or thirteen years past. I have been continually in the business.

Q. Have you worked quite a number of hands?

A. Yes, sir; according to the amount of work being done in the city, I have worked more or less hands.

Q. Have you erected any large heavy buildings, with heavy brick walls?

A. I have never put up any very heavy public buildings. I put up large warehouses.

Q. You have seen large brick buildings built, with heavy brick walls?

A. Yes, sir.

Q. Do you consider yourself a judge of brick work and brick masonry?

A. Yes, sir; I think I am qualified to judge of the quality of a brick wall.

Q. I will ask you if you have examined the work upon the new State House here?

A. I was over there to-day.

Q. How much were you over it, and what means did you have to look at it?

A. The means I had was, by walking around the dffferent parts of the wall; I saw several holes in the walls and places where bricks had been pulled out, and where brick had been taken off the upper portion of the wall.

Q. Did you go into the sub-basement and examine it there?

A. No, sir; I did not.

Q. Give your judgment of the character of—

A. The character of the work I saw I would pronounce good.

Q. You may state to the committee if you looked at all the wall—that is, upon the basement there.

A. I did not examine it minutely. I just walked around the different places, and examined it as I passed round.

Q. Did you examine at those holes in the wall?

A. Yes, sir.

Q. Did you examine that carefully?

A. Yes, sir; then I took my pen knife and picked into the wall, into the crevices and joints. The walls are all well put up, the brick well embedded, and the mortar I consider was good.

Q. Do you regard those walls as safe, to go ahead and build on?

A. I do. some parts of the wall, where it has been frozen—which does not extend far into the walls—but where it has been frozen I think it would be well enough to pull off the several courses of brick there, and put it up again—that is, upon the top of the wall.

Q. The top ought to be taken off so far as the frost extends?

A. Yes, sir; I don't think it would go more than three or four courses of brick at any place, and it don't exist in all parts of the wall.

Q. When those holes were cut into the wall you could look at the character of the work and the character of the mortar to better advantage, could you not?

A. Yes, sir.

Q. Did you or not observe a large hole in the west or southwest part of the building, to the right as you go into the corridor from the north?

A. I presume that is the portion of the building; there is one hole larger than the other, which is upon the west side, I think.

Q. Did you look carefully at that?

A. Yes, sir; quite carefully.

Q. You say the work was good there?

A. The work, at that point, was not quite as good as at the smaller hole; it had not been filled up thoroughly; there were one or two little places there, but that happens in the very best of work frequently.

Q. About how long would it take the mortar to dry, in those heaviest walls?

A. I could not answer that question, positively; but the thicker the wall, the longer it takes the mortar to set in the center; it takes much longer to set in mortar than in cement. I should judge that in some of those walls, unless it was very dry weather, if there were rains every once in a while, keeping the outside of the walls wet, with frequent rains, it might take the walls a year or a couple of years to become thoroughly hardened.

Q. If the brick were wet before they were laid up, would it take a longer or shorter time for them to harden?

A. It would take longer to harden; that is why we wet bricks to make a better job. The slower the mortar hardens, the better work it makes; when brick are not wet in hot weather, sometimes in a few minutes after the brick touches the mortar it will dry out, and then it never sets well.

Q. Suppose those walls were laid along in August, September and on until Christmas, last year, will they not continue to harden, it may be for some years to come?

A. Yes, sir.

By Mr. McMillan:

Q. What length of time is required to thoroughly season and harden those walls?

A. I could not answer that, positively. It might possibly be a year and it might take two years. I have never taken the pains to investigate that; I have never been called upon to investigate how long it would take mortar to harden in a thick wall of that kind.

Examination by Mr. Roberts, Chairman of the committee.

Q. Did you examine the mortar, particularly, in those walls, particularly in the west wall, which had the large hole in it?

A. As I stated before, I did not examine the mortar very minutely. I first gave it a look as I passed around the wall, penetrating the joints with my pen knife; I was careful to examine the mortar at those holes.

Q. Did you examine the sand there?

A. No, sir, I didn't examine the sand; I saw by the character of the mortar that it is a finer sand than we have at St. Louis. It is something like the sand used in the erection of the Governor's mansion, at Jefferson City.

Q. In the other parts of the wall how did you find the mortar?

A. Some of it was done with cement; I think that is harder than the other. Down at the bottom of the work, down at the floor, some of the joints are frozen slightly, but which only goes in about a half inch, not deeper than that; I examined some places where the outside was hard, but as I would penetrate into it it would get softer.

—13

Q. Did you take any of the mortar out and test it, to see whether it had set?

A. Only as I dug it out in penetrating it with my knife.

Q. How large is your knife?

A. [Witness exhibits the knife.] It is about an inch and a half long—the blade.

Q. Could you tell how far that frozen mortar extended in?

A. I don't think it extended more than half an inch or an inch. I dug in beyond where it was frozen; I found it there, after fitting in some little distance, as I suppose is the case with the whole wall. When I got in beyond the hard crust outside, I found it was softer, and judged it would continue so clear through the wall.

Q. Is that the way you would expect to find it?

A. Yes, sir; if the brick had been laid up wet, and with frequent rains, while the work was in progress.

JAMES APPLEYARD, sworn, and examined by Mr. ROBINSON, on behalf of the State House Commissioners:

Q. Where do you reside?

A. In Detroit, Michigan, at the present.

Q. What is your business?

A. I am a practical builder.

Q. How long have you been engaged in that business?

A. I have been engaged upon fire-proof work for some fifteen years. I built the Milwaukee Custom House and Postoffice, and the one in Chicago.

Q. Any other public buildings?

A. Yes, sir, the United States Court House, at Baltimore, and I just finished the new city hall in Detroit—a building costing $500,000.

Q. What did those other buildings cost?

A. I think the one in Chicago cost $365,000. It was built in cheap times. The one in Milwaukee cost about $220,800.

Q. State to the Committee if you regard yourself as a judge of brick work—of masonry.

A. I do consider myself as such.

Q. Will you state whether you have ever examined the work upon the new State House here?

A. I have. I was out there to-day. I didn't know for what purpose.

Q. How long were you there, and how much examination did you make?

A. I went through the building at large—that is, I went thro' the sub-basement, the cellar and basement story, and examined the work. My opinion was asked what I thought of the work. I told them I thought it was a very good piece of work.

Q. Have you examined it sufficiently to give an opinion satisfactory to yourself as to its quality?

A. Yes, sir.

Q. What is its quality?

A. It is good work. Any one who says it is not does so because he don't know anything about it.

Q. Would you say, as a practical man, those walls are sufficient to continue the building, and be perfectly safe?

A. Yes, sir, in every particular.

Q. Did you examine the quality of the mortar?

A. I did.

Q. How did you find it?

A. I found it good.

Q. Did you examine those holes cut in the walls?

A. Yes, sir, I did.

Q. Did you examine the work carefully there, and the character of the mortar?

A. Yes, sir. I found the walls are thoroughly built and grouted as well as it can be done. Of course the mortar was not hard—and it won't be until the building is roofed and fire put into it. Those heavy walls—there is so much moisture in them. I suppose they wet the brick when they were laid—if not, they ought to have done so.

Mr. Robinson:

They were thoroughly wet.

Witness:

You get such an amount of material together that the moisture has got to evaporate in some way before it will dry and harden. For instance—it was three years last April since we commenced our city hall, at Detroit, and until within the last month, when they got fire into it, (they had no fire in it before,) every time there was a warm day outside the building, inside would sweat so you could wipe the water right off the wall and off the iron work and columns, and upon the marble tile it was the same way, and the water would drop from the ceiling; but so long as it was cold and dry outside you could see no water; but the moment there was a warm day it began to sweat. You will find in the erection of these buildings it will remain so until all the moisture is out of the walls. Where there is cement used it will harden quicker than lime. The lime is stronger.

Q. Lime will make stronger walls in the end, will it not?

A. It will make just as strong and as good work for anything above ground.

Q. Then it is your judgment that this is a good job of work?

A. I say it is a good piece of work in every respect.

Examination by Mr. Roberts, Chairman of the Committee:

Q. Did you examine the mortar in those places where holes were cut in the walls?

A. I did.

Q. Did you examine the sand and lime?

A. Yes, sir. Of course there is loam in that sand. It is not probably as good sand as we get in Chicago—it is sharp sand that we get there; it makes a better and stronger mortar.

Q. Is it possible to make as good character of mortar out of this sand as it is out of the sand you speak of getting in Chicago?

A. I think it is, with care. There is plenty of lime in this mortar.

Q. Would this sand be as good?

A. It will not harden, probably, as quick—but yet it will make good work in the end for that kind of work.

Q. Will sand with a good deal of loam in it make as good work as clean, sharp sand with no loam in it?

A. I don't know. I use all kinds of sand. You have to take the sand as you can get it, generally. You want me to say whether it will make as good mortar as sharp sand? It will, if there is no quick-sand in it.

A. Then yon don't think it hurts sand to have a mixture of loam in it?

A. No, sir, I don't think it does hurt it.

Q. Then it dosen't make any difference whether the sand, to make good mortar, is clean, sharp sand, or whether it may have a considerable portion of loam in it?

A. I don't know that it does, if there is no quick-sand in it.

Q. What do you mean by quick-sand?

A. Sand that will run when it is made into mortar.

Q. Do not builders prefer clean, sharp sand to that which has loam in it?

A. For plastering purposes they do.

Q. For building?

A. No, sir, I don't know as they do.

Q. You think you can make just as good building mortar out of sand that has loam in it as you can out of clean, sharp sand?

A. Yes, sir.

Q. Do you know anything of the character of the lime used in this building?

A. No, sir.

Q. Did you examine any of the lime used there?

A. No, sir.

Q. Do you know anything about the Lemont lime?

A. No, sir.

Q. Is lime that has a considerable portion of cement in it as likely to make good mortar with this kind of sand as the other lime—quick lime, with good sharp sand?

A. I should think good enough for all practical purposes.

Q. How long should mortar be mixed before it should be laid in the wall?

A. There is a difference of opinion upon that question. Some builders prefer and some architects prefer not to mix the mortar a week or two in advance, to let it do what we call "souring." Some prefer it to stand three or four days, and some want to use it right along. It depends upon the character of the lime somewhat.

Q. Does the character of the sand have anything to do with it?

A. No, sir; I think not.

Q. How long have you resided in Detroit?

A. For the last three years.

Q. Where did you reside before you went there to live?

A. In Rochester, N. Y. We built the asylum at Batavia.

Q. Were you the contractor?

A. No; the superintendent.

Q. Were you the contractor of the post office in Chicago?

A. No, sir; I was superintendent of that. I was a partner in the building of the Baltimore post office and the city hall at Detroit.

WEDNESDAY MORNING, *May* 31, 1871.

WILLIAM A. STEELE, sworn.

Direct Examination—By Mr. ROBERTS.

Q. What is your name, and where do you live?

A. William A. Steele. I live at Joliet.

Q. Your business?

A. Quarryman.

Q. Have you been in business with any body?

A. I have been in a firm composed of Lorenzo P. Sanger, Wm. A. Steele and Henry A. Sanger.

Q. How long have you been in the business?

A. Since early in 1867.

Q. Have you ever had anything to do with furnishing stone for the State House?

A. Yes, sir; I got one contract. I offered to bid also for the first story.

Q. Were those bids made at public lettings or at private?

A. They were both public, I think.

Q. Who were they made by—yourself?

A. Yes, sir.

Q. State when it was you were awarded the contract, and all about it.

A. Well, I don't know. I believe it must have been about January, 1870, we were awarded the contract for the first story.

Q. State the circumstances.

A. There was nothing about it—only there was a letting for the first story. The specification required the heaviest stone, and we were awarded the contract over all others, at 73 cents per foot in the rough.

Q. Where to be delivered?

A. At the penitentiary at Joliet.

Q. Was there any limit to the amount?

A. Yes, sir; to the first store, including the entablature.

Q. You don't remember the time that contract was made?

A. I think it was in the neighborhood of January, 1870.

Q. Who else bid at that time, do you know?

A. I think Edwin Walker.

Q. Do you know what his bid was? Were you present at the time?

A. I was present at the time. I think his bid was 75 cents per foot.

Q. State how much stone you furnished under that contract.

A. Well, sir, I can't give you the amount in feet, but it amounted to $55,000.

Q. You may state if you are still furnishing stone for the State House; and if you're not, what the reason is.

A. The firm furnished no stone since September, 1870.

Q. Did you furnish all the stone under your contract that was received, as fast as it was required?

A. Yes, sir. A great deal of the time had the derrick piled full of stone. They couldn't cut it as fast as we delivered it.

Q. Was there any delay caused by your failure?

A. No, sir. Perhaps there were a few stone. The present warden asked permission, and we waived our right to them for the State House, only claiming our contract price, as an accommodation to him.

Q. Do you know whether there has been any contract since for stone for the State House—if so, state what you know about it?

A. I only know that public report to the House of Representatives, wherein it was stated that a contract was let to Edwin Walker for the entire building. The report of the State House Commissioners says 80 cents a foot.

Q. State what that will amount to as near as you can get it—the stone to finish the State House.

A. (The witness figures a little.) No, sir; I can't answer you.

Q. Now state, if you had an opportunity to bid for the letting of that stone, at what price you would have furnished it.

A. I shall have to decline to answer that question. I wouldn't like to state unless it would be taken as a qualified statement. I could furnish very well at 73 cents the heavier stone. Of course I could have bid less for the light stone—ten or twenty per cent. less.

Q. Had there been a public letting, would you have bid?

A. Yes, sir; I would.

Q. Did you ever make it known to the Commissioners that you were anxious to bid for the stone for the balance of the building?

A. Can't remember, sir; only it is notorious that we bid everywhere for stone.

Q. Is there an abundance of good stone in your quarry ?

A. Enough for twenty State Houses—as fast as it could be got.

Q. State whether or not the stone to be furnished will be of a larger or a smaller class—whether a cheaper rate or less.

A. A considerable percentage less to finish the building than was required up to the first story; the expense of cutting about the same, but the raw material will be of a quality of stone very much easier to quarry, and the quarrymen can sell it at very much less, as I expected to do.

Q As to the character and quality of stone furnished from the Walker quarry as compared with your quarry ?

A. Do you ask the quality ? I haven't the expensive machinery necessary to test the stone myself, but the United States government tested my quarry and Walker's, the prison and Nauvoo, and every stone of consequence in the northwest, with reference to its custom-houses, of which I have built all since those tests were made—all of them everywhere, and the Rock Island arsenal; and now I won't give these papers, but I wish to furnish the reporter with the contents with reference to the test between Walker's quarry and mine:

Walker's Quarry.—Density, 2.4051; crushing force, 38,733; crushing force in lbs., per square inch, 9692; beginning to spawl, 35,000; breaking weight, per transverse strength, 14,400; transverse strength, S–S. W.—4 bdr.

Absorption.—To determine the absorptive property of different stone, the Walker stone was placed on a steam engine, and remained for sixteen days; it was then weighed, and then placed in water, where it remained three days and nights, and was again weighed, with a result as follows: Weight before steeping, 5020 grains; weight after steeping, 5184 grains; increase in weight, 164 grains; increase per cent., 326 grains.

W. A. Steele's Quarry, Joliet.—Density, 2.6440; crushing force in lbs., 58,853; crushing force, in lbs. per square inch, 14,-708; Began to spawl, 57,833; Breaking weight and transverse strain, 15,850; transverse strength, S–S W—4 bdr.

Absorption.—To determine the absorptive properties of W. A. Steele's stone, it was placed upon the boiler of a steam engine and remained for sixteen days. It was then weighed and placed in water, where it remained three days and nights, and was again weighed, with the result here given: Weight before steeping,

56400.5 grains; after steeping, 5800 grains; increase in weight, 159.5 grains; increase, per cent., 2.8 grains.

Q. I will get you to state the relative qualities of this stone as to the expense of dressing.

A. Well, sir; my sincere judgment is that Walker's is considerably harder to dress than mine.

Q. The Commissioners state that it is said the Walker stone is cheaper at 80 cents a foot than the Sanger stone as a gratuity, on account of its greater ease in dressing.

A. I will state that no person, in my opinion, who understands the subject, would ever believe that; it is untrue, absolutely.

Q. You may state what it is worth a foot to dress it.

A. I couldn't answer without considerable calculation. I can tell you what I would furnish the raw material at of the size required.

Q. What would you furnish it at, at the Penitentiary?

A. 60 cts. a foot.

Q. Can you approximate what it would cost to dress the stone of the kind you would furnish?

A. I would rather not try to approximate. I have never studied about it at all. I have never cut any stone at all. I never saw them cut except incidentally at the prison.

Q. Are you of opinion that stone could be furnished at 60 cts. a foot, that it could be then cut so as to be furnished as cheap or cheaper than the Walker stone at 80 cts?

A. Yes, sir; infinitely cheaper.

Q. Would you be willing to furnish it at cheaper rates?

A. I would be willing to furnish it at 60 cts. per foot, and I am confident that would be cheaper than Mr. Walker's stone at 60 cts., but I wouldn't dress it for anything. I do not dress stone.

Q. State whether you have had any experience relative to the quality of dressing stone.

A. Yes, sir.

Q. State the relative expense of dressing different kinds of stone.

A. The opinion universally expressed, is that they can make far more wages bidding by the job—there is no other way of cutting stone. In Chicago and Joliet they have said they could make more wages on our stone than on Walker's or any other.

Q. Were these parties you speak of, in the habit of dressing all kinds of stone?

A. The most intelligent one of them—all I remember—has cut for at least twenty years on Walker's stone, and says he has finally built his own residence from our own quarry. He works by the job, and makes $125 per month, cutting our stone. Any man who has the chance, easily makes from $90 to $110, at Chicago prices for cutting.

Q. Do you know Mr. Gross, the foreman of the Penitentiary yard?

A. Yes, sir.

Q. State whether you ever had any conversation with him as to the quality of this stone.

A. Well, sir, I cannot remember. I never was much with him. Our interests are entirely antagonistic. We are friends, but I cannot remember of any conversation on that subject.

Q. Do you know anything about the offers made in regard to these lettings? Were there any offers made to you—any inducements held out to you at the time you got the contract?

A. I would first say no Commissioners ever held out any inducements.

Q. If there were any offers, state all about it.

A. Well. Mr. Edwin Walker proposed not to bid. It was at the Leland Hotel, about eight or nine o'clock on the morning the bids were opened he proposed if we would give him $10,000 he would not bid.

Q. Did anybody urge you to give it?

A. Mr. Cochrane urged us to pay him the $10,000.

Q. What reason did he give?

A. I can't remember.

Q. Did you do it?

A. No, sir, I declined it.

Q. How long was that before the time that this last contract was made to Walker?

A. I don't remember the time. I should think about a year before I saw the Commissioners' report.

Q. The Commissioners' report was the first you knew of it?

A. Yes, sir.

Q. Was there any trouble in you furnishing the stone—any difficulty in getting your money?

A. None at all.

Q. Did you give bonds ?

A. Yes, sir.

Q. You carried out your contract ?

A. Yes, sir; the last stone furnished the first October, or perhaps the fifteenth; furnished it all up at the time, except what I told you; the contract was complete.

Cross Examination by Hon. J. C. Robinson, *Commissioner.*

Q. You say the contract had been made almost a year before you found it out—with Walker?

A. No, sir, I didn't say so. He asked me how long it was after I got my contract before I heard of this letting. I said it must have been a year.

Q. When was it Walker wanted you to give him $10,000 for him not to bid?

A. It was the very day of the letting of the first story.

Q. In which you got your contract ?

A. Yes, sir.

Q. Did he bid?

A. I understand so. His bid was read off two cents a foot higher than ours. His was seventy-five cents, and mine seventy-three cents. We got the contract without paying $10,000.

Q. Cochrane advised you to give $10,000?

A. Yes, sir, he urged Mr. Sanger and me both.

Q. Where?

A. In the Leland Hotel.

Q. Who was by ?

A. Henry Sanger was present.

Q. Do you remember whether he was present when Mr. Cochrane advised you to give the $10,000 ?

A. Can't remember.

Q. Who was present then ?

A. As well as I can remember, Mr. Sanger was a partner; he notified me he had been urged by Mr. Cochrane; I think it was the very day the bids were opened.

Q. When did this occur?

A. About nine o'clock.

Q. Let me ask you, Mr. Steele, did you bid upon the stone for the foundation to bring it up to the walls ?

A. Yes, sir.

Q. That contract wasn't awarded you ?

A. No, sir.

Q. You got the contract at seventy-three cents for the first story ?

A. Yes, sir.

Q. You can't be mistaken about the time ?

A. I can very easily be mistaken about anything a year or two ago, but I have given you my best belief.

Q. He wanted you to give $10,000—was that the very day or the day before you got the contract ?

A. Yes, sir, about that time.

Q. Were Walker and you both together when the bids were opened in the Commissioners' office ?

A. I think so.

Q. Was there any other bid except Mr. Walker's and this ?

A. I have the impression there were other bids.

Q. Were the bids read publicly, so you all could hear them and see what each one bid ?

A. Every letting I have attended the bids were so opened ; I can't remember about that one particularly.

Q. Do you remember that bidders had to give bonds to comply with their bids if accepted ?

A. Don't remember that ; remember we had to give bond to comply with our bid.

Q. Mr. Steele, don't you know in this contract you got for the stone, you never bid at all to the Commissioners ?

A. I did put in a bid.

Q. Who bid, and where ?

A. I think it was in the Commissioners' room.

Q. Walker and you both bid at $2 a foot; don't you know there was no public letting at all ?

A. I have said I am not certain about being present at the letting of the bids ; I know that I bid.

Q. I tell you again, Mr. Steele, and to refresh your memory I will read to you from the act approved February 28th, 1867, the second section ; [the Commissioner here read the extract referred to,] now, don't you remember you entered into contract with the Penitentiary Commissioners, and gave your bond to them ?

A. Yes, sir ; after the Commissioners of the State House agreed.

Q. Did you have any agreement ?

A. They wrote the papers I had to sign.

Q. Did you enter into contract with the Commissioners and give bond and receive your money?

A. Yes, sir; certainly.

Q. Did you ever have anything to do with the State House Commissioners about stone?

A Yes, sir; as to quality and value.

Q. So far as the contract is concerned, did they ever make a contract—Mr. Bunn, Mr. Beveridge or myself?

A. In writing?

Q. That or anyway.

A. Yes, sir.

Q. Was there anything more than this, that we said to you that your price with the Penitentiary Commissioners was as low as it could be got?

A. Yes, sir, this, I could do nothing with the others because they said this question had to be settled by the State House Commissioners primarily.

Q. All your dealings had been with the Prison Commissioners and not with us?

A. I got the money generally from you.

Q. They paid you.

A. Yes, sir; I think that was the way it was.

Q. About public and private lettings—do you understand the second was advertised like the first?

A. I don't remember.

Q. What do you remember?

A. I mean a day was fixed, and the parties were here, and the subject was settled at that time.

Q. How was it settled?

A. I can't remember.

Q. What called you here?

A. To bid for the stone.

Q. You say Walker wanted you give $10,000, then he would not bid?

A. Yes, sir.

Q. He bid seventy-five and you seventy-three cents, and got it.

A. Yes, sir; I preferred to take my chances.

Q. Do you recollect, after you got the contract to furnish stone of a given thickness, you found a difficulty in getting stone of that thickness, and consented to be taken thinner, it was cut down an inch ar two to accommodate you?

A. No, sir; I don't remember; I know what you refer to—it was cut down.

Q. Was it not done at your instance or request?

A. It was done at our notice, that we could not find that particular size; but before the contract was signed.

Q. You found a difficulty in getting the size.

A. We never had it.

Q. Did you agree to furnish stone of a given thickness?

A. No, sir; the contract had nothing to say with reference to the plan.

Q. Wasn't the thickness of the stone agreed upon?

A. We had that all fixed before the contract was signed; we could not furnish twenty-six inch water tablature; we never had such a stone; I think the water table was changed one inch after we signed the contract; changed to twenty-four or twenty-three; I don't remember.

Q. Do you know what the size of stone to be used in the walls now is?

A. No, sir; I have no accurate knowledge; I have a general idea; my recollection is, that there is nothing like the proportion of large stone in the upper that there is in the lower story.

Q. You say you would furnish at sixty cents; how is the price of stone now compared with what it was last September?

A. I am certain a good deal lower.

Q. Now, than then?

A. Yes, sir.

Q. Didn't you tell us that seventy-three was as low as you could possibly furnish the stone?

A. Don't remember any conversation of that kind.

Q. Don't you remember you and Mr. Sanger were in the office, and you stated you could not furnish it at a cent less; don't you remember?

A. No, sir.

Q. You know Gross, don't you?

A. Yes, sir.

Q. Has he had much experience in the cutting of stone?

A. I think he has; he has worked for me a good deal, and always as a cutter.

Q. I mean as a foreman—a judge of the cutting of stone; is he a good stone-cutter?

A. Very fair; but his mind is warped now in the handling of convicts; that has got him off from the general idea of stone-cutting; his judgment is not as good.

Q. This contract—you had expected there would be a public letting, and you would have had an opportunity to bid; you mean it was not published by advertising.

A. Not exactly; I mean we had the best stone in the State; and it was done without the knowledge of parties interested.

Q. I suppose all bidders would swear the same?

A. There is the test.

Q. Mr. Steele, as to the quality of the stone to stand positive pressure—do you regard that as important for building purposes?

A. I know it is.

Q. Do you know the Sonora stone?—there is some in the foundation.

A. Yes, sir; I have examined it.

Q. Any danger of that stone crushing under a wall sixty-four or seventy five feet high?

A. Well, sir, I examined the stone and handled it a little. If the building were of any hight, the absorptive qualities of the stone would have to be considered.

Q. Do you think there is any danger in this case?

A. I will answer in a minute. (Witness looks at his papers.) No, sir; I don't think it will crush.

Q. Why? Mr. Stèele, the Sonora stone will not stand as much crushing force as the Walker stone!

A. Walker's is a trace stronger.

Q. You don't believe a wall one hundred feet high would crush?

A. I have said the Walker stone was a trace stronger, and I have been speaking of strength; but I don't know about the disintegration.

Q. That has nothing to do with the crushing force, has it?

A. Yes, sir.

Q. A wall of the size of this State House, any danger of that crushing if built of Lemont or Walker stone?

A. Yes, sir; I think there is danger of its disintegrating.

Q. I ask you again: Is there danger of the Walker stone

crushing under a wall the hight of the State House, from the weight upon it?

A. Yes, sir, I do. I do not mean crush; that is the wrong word. Break is the proper word.

Q. It breaks from the pressure on it?

A. Yes, sir.

Q. How many pounds to the square inch will the Walker stone stand before it breaks from positive force?

A. Well; one sample, seven thousand pounds; another that I have read of—it is in the report now—is nine thousand seven hundred.

Q. This wall is to be ninety-five feet. Now, Mr. Steele, where the foundation is as perfect as it can be made, and the wall made perfectly level, does not each square inch bear just the same proportion of weight?

A. No, sir; because the openings affect the pressure a good deal. If there were no doors nor windows, it might be; but sometimes there is a strain laterally.

Q. That makes no great difference.

A. I could answer you much better if you would let me give an example.

Q. We will do that presently. Take a stone a foot square, and saw it in two twelve times, and then twelve times the other way, how many pieces a foot long would it make?

A. I suppose twelve, if I understand.

Q. You saw it in two twelve times this way and twelve times that way, how many pieces would there be a foot long which you could take and make a pile of—how many feet high would it be?

A. It would be one hundred and forty-four inches high.

Q. One hundred and forty-four feet high, Mr. Steele—12x12 =144.

A. We'll take that for granted; its an arithmetical question.

Q. How many pounds would there be on the lower square inch?

A. There would be about one hundred and fifty-nine—no there wouldn't be anything of the kind—the weight of Lemont stone is one hundred and sixty—the lower cubic inch; yes, sir.

Q. Do you think there is any danger of that crushing with one hundred and sixty pounds upon it?

A. No, sir; not if it was sound stone. I will put that in.

Q. You say in one case it bore seven thousand pounds. Now, one hundred and forty-four feet high, and only one hundred and sixty pounds upon it, there would be any danger?

A. No such strain discovered as that in a building with openings.

Q. Have to build it perfect to get seven thousand pounds on the square inch; you mean where the building isn't plumb?

A. No, sir; not necessarily. That would assist in breaking.

Q. Then you think there is danger of a wall ninety-five feet high, of Lemont stone, crushing?

A. Yes, sir; of Walker's quarry. I would like you to take this as a case of architectural interest. This is a question of that character, and I would like to have an example given. It is to illustrate the answer which I have furnished.

Q. I have no objection.

A. It is this: On the lower end of the island of Rock Island there stands the first building ever put up by government there. It is a very beautiful building; fine architecture; well built; of finely finished stone; exquisitely trimmed. I saw it within the last ten days; the ashler was broken in a good many places; some of it is spawled off, destroying the beauty of the surface; in other places, broken right in two; in some places there were three breaks right together; and that was all because it was built of an inferior stone because it could be got cheap.

Q. Your judgment is, that the break to which you refer was caused by the want of resisting power in the stone; power to resist weight?

A. Yes, sir; I know it is that.

Q. Is there great danger now of this stone in the foundation breaking for want of resisting power—Sonora stone, I mean?

A. If you mean its breaking, I think it might; but if you mean danger from breaking, I think it would not endanger the building, for the reason the stone is in the ground and can't get misplaced.

Q. Do you know Mr. Gross' hand-writing?

A. No, sir; I have seen it frequently.

Q. Do you believe that this is his signature? (Showing a paper.)

A. Can't tell.

Q. Do you know Mr. Guidley?

A. Yes, sir; J. G. Guidley, in the stone business; County Clerk. I have sold him stone.

Q. Do you remember what your bid was for the stone in the foundation?

A. Yes, sir.

Q. What was it?

A. I will come within two cents of it; it was between $1 24 and $1 26. If the unreasonable size in the catalogue were brought down, we could furnish it at a much less price.

WILLIAM D. RICHARDSON sworn on behalf of the Commissioners.

Direct examination by Mr. ROBINSON, *Commissioner:*

Q. Where do you reside?

A. In Springfield.

Q. How long have you resided here?

A. Fifteen years.

Q. Have you been a contractor, engaged in building?

A. Yes, sir.

Q. State what kind of experience you have had in building and superintending brick masonry?

A. Well, for the time I have been at work, it has been considerable.

Q. How long have you been at work?

A. Four or five years.

Q. Have you been at it enough to consider yourself a judge?

A. Yes, sir.

Q. Have you examined the brick masonry of the new State House; and if so, when?

A. I have noticed the work as it was going on; and day before yesterday I went there especially.

Q. How often have you seen it during its progress?

A. Once or twice a month, perhaps; and the other day, particularly.

Q. Upon your observation, what is your judgment as to its being a good job or not?

A. I should call it a good job.

Q. Did you examine those holes through the wall?

A. Yes, sir.

Q. Did that give you an opportunity of examining the work?

A. Yes, sir.

Q. And from that you pronounce it a good job?

A. Yes, sir.

Q. Have you measured any part of the brick work?

A. With Mr. Young, I measured one room only, that was to get Mr. Clark's system of measurement—young Mr. Clark.

Q. State to the committee whether you proposed to measure by sections?

A. (The witness here drew a diagram and explained his method of measuring arches and openings.)

Q. Did you examine the specifications?

A. I did, sir.

Q. Was the measurement in accordance with the specifications?

A. Yes, sir.

Q, Did you compare your measurement with his?

A, I checked his figures after we measured the room.

Q. State how they compared.

A. We found in the room we measured, where the wall was nineteen feet three inches high, it was nineteen feet and five inches high, under-measurement of that one particular room.

Q. Did you measure any but the one?

A. Went down in the cellar and measured one er two piers.

Q. How did your measurement and his compare again?

A. You mean as to the number of brick; it compared all right.

Q. Did you look at his books? And did he show you his manner of measurement? State whether you regard it as a fair and correct measurement under the specifications?

A. Yes, sir; I would say it was.

Q. Of course you have not examined the figures to see if they were correct?

A. No, sir, only that one particular room.

Q. Did you go down in the basement? State whether it would be difficult to measure that now?

A. A man couldn't measure this building correctly unless he had the plans, and a man who is conversant with the building, to explain different parts of it.

Q. Can a man, without the plans and a man with him to explain, take a correct estimate?

A. No, sir.

Q. State why.

A. For a number of reasons. For instance, your specifications say that the cubic contents of the wall shall be taken. Now, unless a man knows, he can't tell how the wall was built. For instance; here is the front face of your wall; that course of stone may run in here; *that* may go away there. A man would have to have the section of wall to state the number of brick distinct from the number of feet of stone.

Q. How about the arches?

A. It would be very difficult to measure them—to determine where the arch started—to measure the arch according to rules, from what we call the skew-back.

Q. That is not the same as the spring of the arch?

A. No, sir; that is where the arch starts.

Q. Would there be any difficulty in getting the thickness of the floor—how far it is from the top of the arch?

A. He would have to measure it to get it correctly; unless he was a scientific engineer, and could get it by taking observations; because he would have to get the level right, on top and so on. It would take a scientific engineer.

Q. One man couldn't go there and measure that.

A. He could only approximate it.

Q. Do you know the character of the sand used there?

A. Yes, sir; I have examined the sand as they were hauling it there; some of it is from the river, and some of it from the bank.

Q. Can there be good mortar made from it?

A. Yes, sir.

By Mr. Beveridge, Commissioner:

Q. Do you know what kind of sand the bluff sand is?

A. Yes, sir.

Q. This is a good job.

A. Yes, sir.

Cross-examination by Mr. Roberts:

Q. Your business?

A. Contractor.

Q. Practical builder?

A. Yes, sir; I consider myself so.

Q. Ever learn the business of brick-laying or stone work?

A. No, sir.

Q. Any other kind of mechanical business?

A. Yes, sir; I worked for five or six years in a machine shop.

Q. What kind of machinery?

A. Iron machinery.

Q. Where was that?

A. State of Connecticut.

Q. When was it?

A. From the time I was thirteen until I was about nineteen.

Q. From the time when you were nineteen, up to this time, what business have you followed?

A. On the Wabash railroad until the last six years.

Q. What were you doing?

A. Part of the time clerk, part of the time general passenger agent, part of the time attending to their tracks, etc.

Q. Within the last six or seven years what have you been doing?

A. Contracting.

Q. To do what?

A. All kinds of building work.

Q. What kind of buildings?

A. I did the brick work on the Carlinville court house; I built the Illinois Female College, at Jacksonville, Toledo, Wabash and Western machine shops, at Springfield.

Q. The Wabash and Western road? Did you superintend it?

A. I did. I had the contract for the brick work.

Q. The Carlinville court house?

A. I superintended that myself.

Q. Was that your first job?

A. No, sir; the first job I did after leaving the Wabash Company, was laying the water pipes in Springfield—the first job of brick work was the Carlinville court house.

Q. Did you ever superintend a job of brick work before that?

A. Nothing, only foundations of my own.

Q. That was all the experience you had up to the time you built the Carlinville court house?

A. Well, I have attended to the building of some culverts bridges, etc., on the Wabash road.

Q. Your experience as a practical builder isn't very extensive up to the time you got charge of the Carlinville court house?

A. No more so than any man who has worked as a practical engineer.

Q. Were you educated an engineer?

A. I told you part of the time—part of the time engaged in the construction of parts of the road.

Q. What did the brick work at Carlinville cost?

A. $16 25 per thousand.

Q. The whole job?

A. Somewhere near $120,000 or $130,000.

Q. Didn't it cost a good deal more than the first estimate?

A. No, sir, my contract was $16 25 a thousand for laying brick —I don't know what the original estimate was.

Q. Didn't the Carlinville court house cost more than was expected?

A. Don't know, except as to my own work.

Q. You made an examination one day this week?

A. I did.

Q. These apertures in the wall?

A. I did; it was a good job of masonry.

Q. Did you say they were as good as could be made?

A. That would be a pretty hard matter to say.

Q. Were any of the walls injured in any way?

A. I saw where the clinches of the mortar had come out by the action of the frost, but I saw no walls permanently injured.

Re-direct—By Mr. Robinson, Commissioner:

Q. You were building the Lincoln Monument?

A. Yes sir.

Q. In your judgment, the amount of brick over there—a man making a measurement with no assistance from engineering—how much of a mistake might he make?

A. All the way from 500,000 to 1,500,000.

Q. Would you risk a measurement of that kind?

A. I don't think a man could measure in that way—I know he couldn't.

Re cross-examination—By Mr. Roberts:

Q. Have you studied engineering?

A. I have.

Q. Practiced it—civil engineering?

A. For my own works—for the road, leveling tracks and such things.

Q. Suppose a good civil engineer had an assistant to aid him, could he measure them?

A. No, sir, unless he had some one with him who had a section drawing of the building.

Q. If he had the plans?

A. If those plans were drawn accurately and shown the outside wall he could measure.

Re-direct again—By Mr. ROBINSON, Commissioner:

Q. Do you know Mr. Bolin-Starck?

A. Yes, sir.

Q. What is he engaged in?

A. I think he is coloring up photographs for the Lincoln Monument.

Q. Good engineer or architect?

Q. I don't think he professes to be an engineer or architect—not to me—only a professional painter.

Q. Do you know whether he is a man of integrity or not?

A. I could state a little circumstance myself that would show.

Q. What was it?

A. He came to me and told me he was at work for Mr. Myers and had a draft in one of the banks. Mr. Myers was to pay him. The draft was for fifty dollars. They were going to protest the draft and he wanted it paid. He said he would give me an order on Mr. Myers for it if I would pay it; he would pay me the next day. I did so. I went to Mr. Myers and he showed me a receipt that he had of him, in full, and didn't owe him anything at all.

Q. Was the receipt dated prior to his representations to you?

A. Yes sir. I then went to Mr. Starck about it, and told him about some matters in Philadelphia I had found that morning. He then gave me his note and promised to pay, but he never has done it.

Re-cross-examination again—By Mr. ROBERTS:

Q. When was this?

A. I should think a year ago.

Q. Some trouble between Myers and Bolin-Starck?

A. I think not; have seen them together.

Q. Any trouble between you and him?

A. No, sir, none at all.

Richard Young sworn—

Direct—By Mr. Robinson, Commissioner:

Q. Where do you reside?

A. In Springfield.

Q. How long have you lived here?

A. Fifteen years.

Q. What business?

A. Bricklaying and plastering.

Q. Are you a bricklayer by trade?

A. Yes sir.

Q. Do you regard yourself as understanding the business?

A. Yes sir.

Q. Have you examined the new State House during the progress of the work?

A. I have been there very frequently.

Q. Have you examined it within the last two or three days?

A. Yes sir, two or three times—I have examined the mortar and brick.

Q. Do you regard it as a good job?

A. Yes sir, I regard it as a good job.

Q. First class?

A. I should call it a first class job—never have seen anything better.

Q. Seen a good deal of brick work?

A. Yes sir.

Q. State whether you have examined the mortar, as to whether the bricks were well imbedded or not?

A. Yes sir, the mortar is spread, and the brick drove down into it.

Q. Have you examined the grouting?

A. Yes sir.

Q. Walls perfectly sound?

A. Yes sir—take off a couple or three courses.

Q. Do you know what kind of sand is there used?

A. I have used it ever since I have been in the city—used it on this building (referring to church in which the House was holding session); this is the same kind of sand.

Q. Can good mortar be made out of that?

A. Yes sir; same kind used on this building.

Q. Did you use the bank sand or river sand on this building ?

A. The trustees thought they would mix it. I showed them the bank sand was the best; the river sand has more loam in it. There is some brnk sand where there is a good deal of loam in it, but not this.

Q. Did you notice the sand as it was being hauled there ?

A. Yes sir.

—

GEORGE PIPE, sworn, and examined, on behalf of the Commissioners, by MR. ROBINSON, as follows :

Q. Where do you reside?

A. In St. Louis.

Q. How long have you resided there ?

A. I have lived there twenty-six years.

Q. What is your business?

A. Brick layer and contractor.

Q. How long have you been engaged in that business ?

A. About forty-one years.

Q. Have you built or superintended any large buildings ?

A. Yes, sir.

Q. Tell the Committee where, and what buildings.

A. I superintended the erection of the basement of the Post-office and Custom House, at St. Louis. Outside of that I have been, during the last year or so, upon the water works at St. Louis.

Q. Do you regard yourself as a judge of brick?

A. I do, sir. I will tell you for what reason. I have been sent for to do complicated work from St. Louis to New Orleans. They paid me four dollars per hour at the Custom House at St. Louis, to superintend particular work there, and the same upon the Court House, upon fine work there, and in complicated arches in the basement. My business has altogether been in that line, doing the best class of work.

Q. From that you would regard yourself as a good judge of brick work.

A. Yes, sir.

Q. State to the Committee whether you have ever examined the work upon the new State House in course of erection here in Springfield.

A. Yes, sir, I have.

Q. How carefully have you examined it ?

A. Well, I went and looked over it thoroughly, and examined the inside to see how it was done. I did not come here with that view. I just happened here, and wanted to look at the work. I thought the work as second to none I had ever seen, in general appearance, everything considered. The bed line is true, and for solidity could not be surpassed.

Q. Have you examined it sufficiently to satisfy your own judgment as to the quality thoroughly.

A. Yes, sir, I have.

Q. Did you examine where those apertures were made in the walls ?

A. Yes, sir.

Q. Did you examine the one upon the west side of the corridor as you go in from the north, upon the right side, a large aperture ?

A. Yes, sir, I looked at it.

Q. Did you examine there as to whether the mortar was good ?

A. I thought the mortar was the best I had ever seen.

Q. Your judgment is that it is second to no job you have ever seen in strength and solidity.

A. Yes, sir.

Q. Do you regard those walls as perfectly safe to go on and erect that building upon ?

A. Yes, sir, perfectly safe, except the top. About three courses of brick should be taken off the top, where the frost has affected it. Thick walls, like that, retain the moisture longer than thin walls, and prevents the frost having any effect upon it, only upon the surface, and that can be easily brushed off, and then it is better than it can be in thick walls. I would take off about three course of brick from the top of the walls, where it has been affected by the frost.

Q. How long would it take mortar to become thoroughly hard in those thin walls where that large hole is cut ?

A. It would take, in a wall like that, a year, or even more, for there is no chance for it to dry thoroughly. That building will sweat from those walls after it is plastered a year, unless it is dried by artificial means. In light walls, if the mortar is dried, you can take your knife and break through the crust and you will find the sand will run. There is no strength to it at all.

Q. You regard this mortar as good as any you ever saw?

A. Yes, sir, I never saw any better.

Q. What was it worth last year, to put that brick in the wall in the manner in which you see it, the man doing the work finding everything?

A. I would hate to do it for $18 00 per thousand, for the cement work, and $15 00 per thousand, for the mortar work. We had $21 00 for the same kind of work.

Examined by MR. ROBERTS, for the Committee:

Q. How long have you lived in St. Louis?

A. Since 1844. I was in Iowa three years of the time.

Q. How old are you?

A. My age is fifty-one years. I was born in the business I have followed, and never left it.

Q. You have examined this mortar and lime?

A. Yes, sir.

Q. Did you examine the sand out of which it was made?

A. Yes, sir.

Q. What do you think of that kind of sand?

A. I think that kind of sand will make good mortar. I saw two kinds of sand. I examiued both piles of sand.

Q. Did you examine that light sand?

A. Yes, sir, I think they can make good mortar of that if they will wash it. I don't think it makes as good mortar as that yellow sand, but it would make good mortar if washed.

Q. Do you know what kind of sand that mortar in the walls was made of?

A. No, sir, I do not.

Q. Did you examine all the walls in the building?

A. Yes, sir.

Q. When did you examine them?

A. Last Saturday a week.

Q. How long have you been in the city?

A. Only since yesterday.

Q. Did you examine it since you have been in the city this time?

A. No, sir.

Q. How long were you engaged in examining it.

A. Just long enough to look over it—two or three hours.

Q. Had you ever been in the building before?

A. No, sir.

Q. Were you ever in Springfield before?

A. Once.

Q. At whose instance did you examine it?

A. Not by anybody's. I came to look at it from curiosity. I was at Jacksonville and came over here. I never spoke to Mr. Piquenard or anybody else. I am a stranger here.

Q. At whose instance did you come to-day?

A. At Mr. Piquenard's, who was with me when I made the examination.

Q. What business are you engaged in now?

A. I am doing nothing.

Q. How long have you been engaged in that business?

A. About a week or ten days. I got through with the water works. I am looking for business now, and will not be long without it. I want to take a little recreation, as I have been closely confined for a long while.

Q. Did you examine the stone work upon the building?

A Yes, sir, I looked at it as I passed through the building. My remark was, directly after I ssw it, that it was a very fine job.

Q. You would not have been willing to take that job of brick work for less than $15 per thousand?

A. I don't know what brick is worth bere, but I would want $8 upon the price of the brick for the cement work, and $5 for the mortar.

Q. Over and above the cost of the brick?

A. Yes, sir.

F. Schroeder sworn, and examined on behalf of the Commissioners by Mr. Robinson.

Q. Where do you reside?

A. In Chicago.

Q. How long have you resided there?

A. Nine years next August.

Q. What is your business ?

A. Brick mason and builder.

Q. How long have you been engaged in that business?

A. About twenty-nine years now; probably a little more.

Q. Do you consider yourself a judge of brick masonry ?

A. Yes, sir, I do.

Q. Have you ever superintended the work upon any large building with heavy walls?

A. Yes, sir, I have.

Q. Where?

A. In Chicago. For instance, the *Tribune* building.

Q. Have you worked any upon the new State House here ?

A. Yes, sir, I have.

Q. In what capacity ?

A. I acted as foreman of the brick work ; was done when you came here. There was a start made upon the west side or the southwest. Three piers or four were built up to the spring of the arch, there where the south and west end joins together. The walls of the cellar were built.

Q. Now state to the Committee whether you superintended the building of the balance of the brick wall ?

A. I did, sir.

Q. Were you there daily and hourly ?

A. I was there from seven o'clock in the morning until six in the evening, the whole day.

Q What was your business ? Was it to watch the entire work ?

A. My business was to watch the brick work, and see that it was done.

Q. Who employed you ?

A. Mr. Barnard.

Q. If he gave you any direction about the work being well done, and not allow it to be slighted, state it to the Committee.

A. Yes, sir. Mr. Clark gave me the specifications, and instructed me to carry the work out in accordance with them. I had the same instructions from Mr. Barnard.

Q. State to the Committee the *modus operandi* of laying the brick, how the mortar was laid, and whether the bricks were wet?

A. The mortar was made partly of cement and partly of lime, and about four parts of sand. It was said it should have been made five parts of sand, but it could not be used. It made the mortar too poor. We had such close joints we could not add the sand called for by the specifications.

Q. What part of cement did you use?

A. One part of cement, one part of lime, four parts of sand, or something like that.

Q. Go on and state how the brick were prepared for being laid.

A. The brick were wet first. They were thoroughly wet, too much so in my opinion. I was talking to the superintendent and architect, and told them the brick had too much water. The brick layers complained most of the time because the brick was so wet it broke the skin off their hands. We grouted every course thoroughly.

Q. What do you mean by grouting?

A. We generally had a half dozen barrels or so, and had our mortar in there. We put our water into it. We had a gang of men taking it out in buckets, and pouring it on as we needed it.

Q. What was the object of that?

A. To fill up all the apertures.

Q. Did you fill them all up?

A. Yes, sir.

Q. State whether Mr. Clark, the superintendent, was there all the time, or his son?

A. Yes, sir. To my knowledge Mr. Clark or his son were there all the whole day. Sometimes Mr. Clark would be in his office working, but he was generally around there from morning till evening.

Q. Have you examined the work since you came down this time?

A. Yes, sir.

Q. From your examination, state whether that is a good job or not.

A. It is as good a job of work as I ever saw. It is as good a piece of work as I have seen since I have been in the trade. I could never do a better piece of work than we done there.

Q. State whether in your opinion it will be necessary to take two or three course of brick off the top wall and relay it?

A. It appears to me so. Yes, sir, the wall has not been well covered. It was sort of cemented over the top so as to keep it from the weather, but when the ice and snow came upon it, it worked into the wall, and froze it in some places two or three deep, and in some places one course. That is a small matter, and will not injure the wall, the balance of it, at all.

Q. About how many bricks will have to be taken off—take the whole wall?

A. It is hard to say that.

Q. It would not be a large number?

A. No, sir.

Q. When you speak of this being a good job, do you speak of the entire work?

A. Yes, sir.

Q. You regard the walls as being entirely reliable and safe, to go on with the building?

A. I do, sir.

Q. How were the walls backing up against the stone, built? Was that well done?

A. It was done as carefully as any of the rest.

Q. Do you believe the work could have been made any better by any amount of additional care or labor put upon them?

A. No, sir.

Q. Do you regard the cement, the lime and the sand as being good materials?

A. As good materials as ever were used, sir.

Examination by Mr. Roberts on behalf of the committee:

Q. What sort of sand was used in making the mortar of which those brick walls are made?

A. It was of what I understand to be river sand, here.

Q. Was there more than one kind of sand used?

A. Not to my knowledge. The quality may have been a little different, but it was all one kind of sand, as I understand it.

Q. What kind of lime was used?

A. The Walker lime.

Q. Where was it made?

A. At Lemont.

Q. What kind of lime is it—first class lime?

A. Yes, sir.

Q. How long was the mortar made before it was put into the walls?

A. Some of the mortar must have been made three or four days. It is hard to tell, because there is always mortar on hand, and we keep adding to it.

Q. Is it not true that you could not make up mortar and keep it any length of time, because it would set and get hard, because there was so much cement in it?

A. No, sir.

Q. Didn't you have a large amount of lime slacked, and didn't it become hard so you could not use it?

A. That was before I came here.

Q. Didn't you have to make up the mortar and use it the same day?

A. No, sir.

Q. How long does the lime slack before you use it, generally?

A. Three or four days, or some where along there.

Q. You say this injury on the top courses of the walls were done by snow and frost?

A. Yes, sir.

Q. Is it usual, where large buildings are being erected, to have the walls covered in the winter?

A. Yes, sir; they generally cover them up with boards.

Q. You think the ice and snow getting upon those walls did not hurt them?

A. No, sir, I think not; except on the top.

Q. Don't you know that along the doors and windows they are injured as bad as upon the top?

A. I didn't notice it.

Q. Do you think the injury was from the ice, snow and bad weather?

A. Yes, sir.

Re-examined by Mr. Robinson:

Q. Was the lime slacked a sufficient length of time before it was used—before the mortar was used—so as to make it good?

A. Yes, sir.

Q. Would the covering up of that wall, and keeping it covered during the winter, with boards, have cost as much, or more than the taking down and re-laying a few courses of brick?

A. I think it would have cost more to have covered it.

EDWIN WALKER sworn and examined by Mr. ROBINSON on behalf of the commissioners:

Q. Where do you reside?

A. At Lemont.

Q. State to the committee whether you are the owner of the Lemont stone quarry?

A. Yes, sir; I am.

Q. Are you furnishing stone for the erection of the new State House?

A. Yes, sir.

Q. Have you a contract for furnishing stone?

A. Yes, sir.

Q. For what amount of stone have you a contract for furnishing stone to the state?

A. The outer walls of the next two stories.

Q. About how much—how many feet, in the aggregate, will that amount to?

A. About 380,000 feet.

Q. What are you getting from the state for that stone?

A. I am getting eighty cents per cubic foot, delivered at the penitentiary.

Q. With whom did you make that contract?

A. With the penitentiary commissioners.

Q. The present story now built of the State House was built from the quarry of Sanger and Steele?

A. Yes, sir.

Q. Did you make a proposal for that?

A. Yes, sir.

Q. To whom did you make that proposal?

A. With the penitentiary commissioners.

Q. Did you ever put in any bid or proposal in writing for furnishing stone for that to the State House Commissioners?

A. No, sir.

Q. It was all with the penitentiary commissioners?

A. Yes sir.

Q. Did you make any bid for any work to the State House Commissioners?

A. No, sir.

Q. Mr. Steele has stated here that you and he were down here putting in bids for the present story, and that you wanted him to give you $10,000 not to bid? How is that?

A. Mr. Sanger, of the firm of Sanger & Steele, wanted to furnish the stone for the basement. He said he had got the contract—or so good as got it—that there was no chance for me; that there was no use for me to bid, for it would not be considered. Of course, I thought I would make the bid any way, and get it if there was a possible chance. The penitentiary commissioners notified me to make a bid. I sent it down.

Q. Did you ask him to give you $10,000 not to bid?

A. No, sir. He offered to give $10,000 if I would let him make his own price. Mr. Steele was the man who made the arrangement. He said I might as well take the money as not to have anything.

Q. Did he offer you the money.

A. Yes, sir; himself.

Q. Now, let me ask you another question: Have you been approached since you come down here—has a proposition been made to you if you would permit Sanger & Steele to furnish a portion of this stone—that Steele should be sent home, and would not testify before this Committee?

A. Yes, sir; Mr. Sanger gave me a written proposition, if they could furnish one quarter or such a matter of the stone for the building, Steele should come before the Committee and be favorable toward me.

Q. Now, I want to ask you another question: What were you getting for your stone in the Chicago market, say of the same character you were furnishing for the new State House last year?

A. Different prices. The lowest price was 75 cents per cubic foot, and the highest $1.25.

Q. In point of quality, how did that compare with the stone furnished here?

A. The average price was $1.10. It went according to the bill of prices. I make a publication every year of prices.

Q. Did Sanger & Steele have a bill of prices?

A. I could not tell you.

Q. State to the Committee whether there is any difference in the cutting of your stone and that from the quarry of Sanger & Steele.

A. Yes, sir; a good deal of difference.

Q. What is the difference in dollars?

A. The difference consists in the labor and the forming of the different kinds of work. Sanger & Steele's is a good deal the hardest to cut.

Q. In cutting straight work, what would be the difference per cubic foot—plain, straight work?

A. About forty per cent. in plain work.

Q. When it comes to carving and the different kinds of moulding, what would it be?

A. That would depend somewhat upon the character of the moulding. In moulding like that upon the upper course of the basement of the new State House, there would be a difference of perhaps $2.50 or $3.00 per running foot. That is pretty heavy moulding.

Q. If you take the opinion of stone, have you ever talked to stone cutters upon the subject as to whether this would make any difference?

A. Yes, sir; I talked to them two or three years ago, when they were working out estimates. I talked to Mr. Gindele, and Went, and Messenger, and one or two others.

Q. What were their opinions upon it?

A. It was that they would not use the Sanger & Steele stone at all, if they got the work, unless the State compelled them.

Q. Have you talked to Mr. Gross upon the subject—Mr. Gross of the Penitentiary?

A. Yes, sir; his judgment was there would be from $40,000 to $50,000 difference in the cutting, for the whole building.

Q. Are you a stonecutter?

A. I am.

Q. What is your judgment of it?

A. That would be my judgment.

Q. You have been burning the lime used in the new State House?

A. Yes, sir; I have been burning lime for two years—this is the third season.

Q. Have you ever burned lime at Lemont, before that?

A. No, sir; there was a company there, some 16 or 17 years ago, burning from the top rock. We are burning, now, thirty feet down from the surface.

Q. Is your lime generally used in this country now?

A. Yes, sir.

Q. Can you name some of the companies using your lime?

A. Yes, sir: Grant & Wilson use it entirely; they use none other. Potter Palmer used it in his hotel—the large one he built last summer—and will use it in his new hotel, now in process of erection.

Q. Is the hotel he is building to be a very extensive building?

A. Yes sir, it is to be entirely fire-proof, and will cost in neighborhood of $1,500,000.

Q. Name some other firms, if you remember them.

A. Henry Onery used it in his building upon the corner of Dearborn and Monroe streets, Chicago—a five-story marble building.

Q. Who was the architect of that building?

A. Mr. Wheelock. The court house in Chicago—the new extension of it—was built with that lime; Mr. Loburg uses it entirely; Messrs. Steele & McMahan use it.

Q. Give the committee some idea of the quantity you sell of your lime.

A. Last year we sold 40,000 barrels, and the year before 11,000 barrels, and this year I have no doubt we will sell 70,000 to 80,000 barrels.

Q. Are you selling as much as any other in the country, at this time?

A. I believe Stearne & Co. are selling the most in Chicago.

Q. Where is this lime burned?

A. In Chicago, near Bridgeport; they get the stone there.

Q. What is the difference between that and your lime?

A. That lime is a little lighter color and is a softer lime. They use it a good deal for hard-finishing in plastering.

Q. Is your lime regarded as of good quality by those using it?

A. Yes sir.

Q. Do you regard it as first quality lime?

A. Yes, sir—I am positive of it; I have had three years' experience with it.

Q. You spoke something about your price-list. You contracted to furnish this stone, with the Penitentiary Commissioners, for 80 cents?

A. Yes, sir; they wrote me to come down and see what I could furnish stone at, for the next story. I told them that in consideration of the large amount there would be to furnish, I would make a concession, and contracted to furnish it at that price.

Q. How does the stone of the present story of new State House compare in size with that to be furnished upon the next story, leaving out the bottom course.

A. It is to be entirely different. The next story will require heavier stone. A great deal of it is to be four feet, three inches thick, for the plints, offsets, jams and so forth, and are required to be laid upon a natural bed.

Q. Do you know Sanger & Steele's quarry?

A. Yes, sir.

Q. Can they furnish that heavy stone from their quarry?

A. No, sir, they have no layers of that thickness. I furnished the Government of the United States with some stone they contracted for two or three years ago. They could not furnish it. They were at it three years.

Q. Is there any quarry about Joliet having that thickness except your own?

A. No sir, not one. Sanger & Steele come next to ours.

Q. How does your stone compare with Sanger & Steele's in uniformity of color?

A. Mine is more regular. It is all the same from top to bottom. We have only the one kind.

Q. Is it uniform as to hardness or softness.

A. Yes, sir.

Q. How is Sanger & Steele's as to uniformity of color?

A. It is very bad in that respect.

Q. How many builders in Chicago, so far as you know, use stone from Sanger & Steele's quarry, in preference to yours?

A. I can only say that Mr. Sanger commenced a stone yard in Chicago two years ago, and had to quit the yard, and I am now occupying the same yard.

Q. What amount of business are you doing?

A. I am doing an extensive business. I am now working three hundred men at my yard.

Q. Which is used the most extensively in Chicago, your stone or Sanger & Steele's?

A. They don't furnish a foot of stone in Chicago, so far as I know.

Q. Do you furnish a large amount ?

A. Yes, sir, we furnish a large amount—over a thousand feet per day. Potter Palmer contracted for some stone, with the penitentiary, by means of which Sanger & Steele furnished some stone.

Q. You are now speaking of superstructure stone ?

A. Yes, sir, stone for superstructure. Anybody could furnish foundation stone.

Examination by MR. ROBERTS, on behalf of the Committee :

Q. Who was the architect of Potter Palmer's hotel—the one that is built ?

A. Mr. Roberts.

Q. You furnished the stone for that ?

A. Yes, sir. I am also furnishing stone for the foundation of his new one.

Q. You say the stone going upon the upper stories of this new State House is to be larger than that in the basement story ?

A. Yes, sir.

Q. How thick are the walls to be, including the brick and stone—the outside walls.

A. I know nothing about the brick walls. The stone required is to lay upon a natural bed, and has nothing to do with the depth of the wall. The thickness of the wall is another thing. The depth of the stone is the height of the wall, and not the thickness. The stone is laid down the way it grew in the quarry.

Q. When the stone are laying transverse, how deep do they go into the wall ?

A. Some three feet, some three feet six inches, some two feet, some one foot nine inches. I don't know exactly, but they are all to be one particular height.

Q. How high is that ?

A. Some two feet two inches, and some two feet nine and a half inches, a good many of them two feet eleven inches, and three feet four inches.

Q. Is it usual to erect buildings with stone heavier above than below ?

A. Yes, sir, in many buildings the basement story is considered the principal part of the structure, with heavy piers, columns and projections, which require heavier stone. The next story in this new State House will have the heaviest stone. In designs of this kind that is the main story, and requires the heaviest stone on account of the heavy columns, projections, etc., which comes upon that story.

Q. What is it worth per foot to dress this stone of yours ?

A. That depends upon the kind of labor you put upon it.

Q. Plain dressing, I mean, as you dress this.

A. It is worth a dollar to a dollar seventy-five, superficial measurement.

Q. Do you know what the penitentiary is getting for that ?

A. No, sir.

Q. What will the stone cost, after it is dressed, per foot ?

A. About $1 80.

Q. You say this Sanger & Steele stone is not used in Chicago at all, for building purposes?

A. No, sir, it is not.

Q. What is the reason of it ?

A. It is too hard for the manufacturer to make a living at.

Q. You say you never offered Sanger & Steele, if they would give you a certain amount of money, that you would not put in a bid for furnishing stone for this basement story ?

A. No, sir.

Q. Neither to Sanger nor Steele ?

A. No, sir. They tempted me to do it.

Q. Who did that ?

A. Sanger and Steele both, so that they could get about $1 20 per square foot.

Q. You declined to do it ?

A. Yes, sir.

Q. What did you put in your bid at, at that time ?

A. I think at seventy-eight cents, I am not positive.

Q. Was it a sealed bid ?

A. Yes, sir.

Q. Where was it put in ?

A. At Joliet.

Q. Were you here the day the contract was let ?

A. No, sir, I was not. I think I would have got the job if I had been here. I was the lowest bidder, I think.

Q. Who changed the bid ?

A. I don't know, but I was told that I ought to have had the job.

Q. Who told you ?

A. Some parties interested.

Q. Who were they ?

A. I can't tell you now.

Q. Who had the letting of that job ?

A. The Penitentiary Commissioners.

Q. Where was that job let ?

A. At Joliet.

Q. Where did you put in your bid ?

A. At Joliet. I sent my bid down, but ought to have gone down with it. I sent it to Joliet. I was fourteen miles from Joliet at the time, and they telegraphed me for an explanation. It was hard to tell what they meant. I started on my way down the next morning, when I found out it was too late.

Q. When was that conversation you spoke of where it was proposed that Steele would testify favorable for you if you would let him have a portion of the contract ?

A. It was this morning.

Q. Where ?

A. In the Leland Hotel.

Q. Give us the whole conversation.

A. We got to talking about this Investigating Committee, and what we had to do here. I told him my subject was the lime, and had nothing else to do with it. He says : "They are going to smash your contract !" I told them I didn't know about that. I told them I didn't know as it made much difference to me ; not so much as to them, as I could sell lots of my stone. Steele was going to testify, and was going to tell all about the transaction we had. He was going to open the whole thing. I said : "Well, you said the job was yours, and if you could make more money out of it you would give it to me. You have got the job, and that is all there was about it." He then proposed that I should give him about a quarter of this present contract, or as much as they could furnish, or not any if they thought not proper to furnish any, and he would recommend Steele to go off upon the next train. He then pulled out this written paper, specifying what they should do, or might do ; and said if I would sign it, it would be all right. I didn't say whether I would sign it or not.

Q. Have you got that written paper?

A. No, sir; he has it in his possession. He wrote out the proposition last night.

Q. Did you have any conversation with the Penitentiary Commissioners, or any others, before you got this last contract, as to what you would bid, or was it a sealed bid?

A. It was a sealed bid. They asked me if I could furnish stone according to the plans and specifications of the architects.

Q. Did you make a sealed bid?

A. Yes, sir.

Q. Was there any other bid but yours?

A. Not that I am aware of.

Q. Who notified you to make a sealed bid?

A. The Penitentiary Commissioners.

Q. Do you know whether they notified anybody else?

A. I don't know.

Q. Were any bids read with yours?

A. I don't know.

Q. Did they know what you were going to bid before the bid was opened?

A. No, sir.

Q. When was that bid put in?

A. In August or September.

Q. You had no conversation with anybody else about what they were going to bid?

A. No, sir.

Q. The Penitentiary Commissioners didn't know what it was until it was opened?

A. No, sir.

Q. Were you there when it was opened?

A. I don't remember.

Q. How long after the bid was made did you get the contract?

A. Probably two weeks. It was two or three weeks before they ordered me to go along.

Q. Did you enter into the contract at that time?

A. Yes, sir.

Q. A written contract?

A. Yes, sir.

Q. And gave bonds for the performance of it?

A. Yes, sir.

William Sands, sworn and examined, on behalf of the Commissioners, by Mr. Robinson.

Q. Where do you reside?

A. In the city of Springfield.

Q. How long have you resided here?

A. For twenty years.

Q. What has been your business since your manhood?

A. Building and superintending work. I have done a great deal of superintending, in the city of Springfield, in the constructing of sewers and buildings.

Q. How long have you been engaged in that business?

A. When I was fourteen years of age I went to my trade then.

Q. Did you learn a trade?

A. Yes, sir; I served an apprenticeship of seven years, in New York City, and got my diploma at the expiration of the seven years. In the days when I served my time, we learned everything. The boss would put us in the cellar, first laying stone, and then he would put us on the brick work, and then at plastering. We worked through everything before our trade was complete.

Q. You have superintended brick masonry a good deal, have you?

A. Yes, sir.

Q. Do you regard yourself as a good judge of brick masonry?

A. I have seen enough of it, and handled enough of it; I should think I ought to be.

Q. Do you think you are?

A. Yes, sir.

Q. Have you noticed the brick work upon this new State House, at different times?

A. I should say I saw it twice a week; probably more.

Q. Did you notice how the work was done, as it went on?—have you examined it as far as it is done?

A. Yes, sir. I examined the work a half dozen times thoroughly.

Q. State whether it is a good job, according to your judgment.

A. I have been up there since there has been a good deal of conversation about it. I have taken pains to get hard brick out—tried to break the brick out of the wall, while the work was going up. I thought it was a "tip top" good job, good work, good materials and everything good—more particularly from the fact that there is a "heading" every second course—they could not do that without grouting the whole thing.

Q. Did you note whether the bricks were well bedded in the mortar?

A. Yes, sir; I noticed that frequently. They are well bedded in the mortar.

Q. What was the quality of the mortar.

A. It was as good mortar as I ever saw go into a building.

Q. Do you regard it as a good job?

A. I count those walls upon the new State House as good as I ever saw.

Q. Have you had some experience in measuring brick walls?

A. Yes, sir.

Q. Were you with young Mr. Clark and some other gentlemen in measuring some of those walls?

A. Yes, sir.

Q. How many and what part of the walls did you measure?

A. We went over there and the young man, Clark, told us to select any of the rooms and measure them. The first wall we measured was the long wall in the hall. Mr. Richardson held the tape-line upon the bottom, and Mr. Young upon the top. It measured nineteen feet and five inches. Mr. Clark turned to his figures and found he had made it nineteen feet and three inches. We tried the tape-line upon several places—not knowing his figures—and found the measurements in accordance with the figures put down upon his book.

Q. Do you mean to say you made a calculation to see if they agreed with his figures?

A. Yes, sir. They agreed—at least ours run over his a little.

Q. Did you measure any in the cellar?

A. Yes, sir, we measured the arches as well as we could.

Q. How did they come out where you measured?

A. They come out about as his figures are.

Q. I want your opinion, whether a man can go there without the plans, and measure that work correctly—the arches and everything?

A. No, sir, it is impossible for a man in Springfield, or in the State of Illinois, to do that and do justice between man and man, without a skeleton plan to do it by.

Q. Might he not make very serious mistakes in the number of bricks—could he help making mistakes?

A. A man could not carry the tape line around and measure those arches correctly, at all. He must have details to do it.

Q. Have you been using this same kind of sand in the city here for a good many years?

A. Yes, sir, for twenty years.

Q. Does it make good mortar?

A. It will make as good mortar as any sand. I finished Col. Williams' bank here, about fifteen or sixteen years ago, and used that same sand as they are using in the new State House.

Q. In your judgment, can you make as good mortar and as good work out of that sand as the sand they use in Chicago?

A. Yes, sir, I think I could.

Examination by Mr. Roberts, on behalf of the Committee.

Q. Can a man measure that if he has somebody with him to hold the tape if he has the plans along with him?

A. I don't think he could do it correctly—the stays and everything is in the way there, and he could not get at it.

Q. You think it can not be measured at all now, do you?

A. No, sir, it can't be done without knowing something about the figures.

Q. Suppose a man takes the skeleton plans of the building and takes somebody along with him to hold the tape line, if he is a good mathematician and a good engineer, can't he measure those walls?

A. No, sir.

Q. Is there no way it can be measured?

A. He can measure them with the plans.

Q. I say if he takes the plans and somebody with him to hold the tape line?

A. No, sir, not without he has somebody to tell him how the walls are; there is one stone there projecting probably six inches, and another may be twelve inches, and another four inches. Nobody could measure the building without he had somebody to tell him about the stone there. If he had somebody to tell him the size of all the stone in the building he might then measure it.

Q. That is the only way?

A. Yes, sir, no man can do it, I think, in any other way.

Q. Have you noticed the sand out of which that mortar is being made in that building?

A. Yes, sir, I have.

Q. What kind of sand is it?

A. The majority of it is river sand.

Q. Where did they get it?

A. In the Sangamon river.

Q. What is the color of that sand?

A. It is called the grey sand; there is another sand out there, (this coarse bluff sand) which is called as good as the other.

Q. Is there any loam in that?

A. No, sir.

Q. What color is that?

A. A light yellow.

Q. Is that as good sand as any other?

A. Yes, sir.

Q. Will it make as good mortar?

A. Yes, sir.

By Mr. Robinson:

Q. You know what kind of sand this church (meaning the hall of representatives) was put up with?

A. Yes, sir; it was the bluff sand; the same kind as that in the State House yard.

By Mr. Roberts:

Q. What kind of lime was used in this church?

A. I think it was Indiana lime—I am not positive.

Alfred H. Piquenard sworn, and examined on behalf of the Commissioners—

By Mr. Robinson:

Q. Where do you reside?

A. In Springfield, now.

Q. What is your profession?

A. I am an architect.

Q. How long have you been in that business?

A. I could not say. Since I was a man I have always followed it. Never did anything else, except when I was a soldier. I have followed it in this country since 1854.

Q. Did you follow it in France?

A. Yes, sir: engineering more than architecture; my father was a builder.

Q. Are you the architect of the new State House here.

A. I am.

Q. You and Mr. Cochrane are partners?

A. Yes, sir.

Q. Explain to the committee whether there have been any changes made in the plans of the building since your and Mr. Cochrane's plans were reviewed by Carter & Dykeman, architects at Chicago.

A. Yes, sir, a few little changes have been made.

Q. What are they?

A. We diminished some of the brick work in opening the wall to the hall in the basement so as to give more light in the halls.

Q. What other changes?

A. We took off the iron beams and replaced them with brick arches.

Q. Any other changes?

A. We took off the steps upon the north and south entrances. I don't know of any more changes of importance. A door may have been moved a little here or there, one way or the other.

Q. Was there not a change in the dome?

A. Yes, sir; we diminished the thickness of the walls of the dome.

Q. In your judgment, as an architect, are the brick arches equally as good in the basement or cellar as the iron beams would have been?

A. Better, in one respect. The reason we advised the change was, it was more economical; and in the second place, iron beams in a cellar of a public building, after a certain time, may rust when nobody would suspect it or look for it. If the rust is not scraped off after it begins, it will accumulate so, that in the course of twenty or twenty-five years, the beams would be dangerous.

Q. For that reason you regard the brick arches as the safer and the better of the two?

A. I did.

Q. Which would cost the most?

A. The iron beams would cost the most.

Q. About what amount?

A. The iron beams would cost about $10,000, that is, the iron alone; but if brick were put between the iron, that would cost about $4,000, making the whole cost $14,000 more than the arches.

Q. You spoke of a change in the dome; what was that change?

A. We diminished the thickness of the wall of the dome.

Q. Is that a saving or a loss to the State?

A. A saving to the State.

Q. How much, about?

A. I suppose it would save nearly 20,000 cubic feet of stone; that stone would cost us here $25,000 or $30,000.

Q. The changing of iron to be used in the dome, from stone—will that be as good in that part of the building as stone?

A. Fully as good.

Q. Which will be the cheaper of the two?

A. The iron would be cheaper; the iron that we use there is so slight and strong, that the comparison could not be made scarcely; if the stone cost $1,000, we could replace it with iron for $100, making a difference of $900.

Q. What is your judgment of the adopting the iron for the stone? How much will it save to the State?

A. It will save about $20,000.

Q. Now, let me ask you, has there been any change made in the plans since they were supervised and looked over by the architects alluded to, that will make the building cost any more?

A. No, sir; there will be a saving of about $80,000 upon the basement, as I calculate it; about $20,000 of which it is proposed to put in these walls, lining them with stone instead of plastering, making it firmer than we originally intended by the plans.

Q. What I want to get at is this, whether, in your judgment, any change has been made in the plans that will make the building cost more than was contemplated by the plans looked over and examined by those architects in Chicago?

A. No, sir; none at all.

Q. Did you assist in making the plans and specifications that were adopted by the Legislature?

A. Yes, sir.

Q. Did you assist in making those looked over by the architects?

A. Yes, sir.

Q. What was your estimate for that?

A. Besides what was already expended, $2,000,600 and some odd thousand dollars; I cannot give you the exact figures without reference to books.

Q. What was their calculation?

A. It was some $85,000 more than our estimate.

Q. But still under $3,000,000.

A. Yes, sir.

Q. What is your opinion upon the cost of the completion of the building; in your judgment can it be completed within that amount of money, according to the plans and specifications?

A. Yes, sir; it can.

Q. Do you know of any responsible parties who are willing, or who have expressed a willingness to take the contract and build it for that amount of money?

A. Yes, sir; Col. Williams, of this city, and a company are willing to take the contract and finish the building for the limit fixed in the Constitution.

Q. Any other parties?

A. They are the most responsible parties; these parties can furnish ample security; the others who would accept it might not be able to do so; I know of many others who would be willing to do it; I would be willing to take it myself if I could furnish the security, and I think I could furnish the security, but would not swear to that now; it would be a large amount.

Q. Who furnished the stone for the basement story of the new State House?

A. Sanger & Steele, of Joliet.

Q. Have you examined their stone quarry?

A. Yes, sir; pretty closely.

Q. State whether there was any difficulty in getting them to furnish that stone as to quantity or quality, or anything else.

A. Our first design was for stone twenty-eight inches in thickness for the first course; we found that there was but one quarry where they could furnish it that thickness; we advised the Commissioners, and with the Penitentiary Commissioners, and changed our plans; Sanger and Steele promised us certainly to furnish stone twenty-five inches in thickness, if we would change the plans by diminishing it to twenty-five inches; we did so in order that we could get competition; we thought it was for the interest of the State that we should diminish our plans from twenty-eight to twenty-five inches for the base course, and did so because by doing so we made competition with other quarries.

Q. Was that done to accommodate Sanger & Steele?

A. Yes, sir; so as to have competition with other quarries, as there was but one quarry that could furnish twenty-eight inches, which was Walker's; after we went to the trouble of changing the plans, the Penitentiary Commissioners made a contract with Sanger & Steele; and then after they got the contract they asked us to change the plans from twenty-five to twenty-four inches, because they could not furnish twenty-five inches; after all they didn't furnish twenty-four inch stone, but had to buy it—at least nine-tenths of it.

Q. Do you know of whom they bought the stone?

A. They bought it from Mr. Knobe's quarry, from which they could have furnished twenty-eight inch stone.

Q. State whether there was any difficulty in getting stone of uniform color?

A. There was some difficulty, but I must say that as a general thing we had better stone than I expected.

Q. Do you recollect at one time, about the Commissioners being at the Penitentiary examining the stone?

A. Yes, sir; I was there present; we had some difficulty, but would expect to have that with any quarry.

Q. You may state to the committee, whether there was, so far as you know, any public letting or receiving of bids by the Commissioners of the new State House, for the stone for the basement?

A. No, sir; there was not.

Q. The contract, you say, was with the Penitentiary Commissioners.

A. Yes, sir; between the Penitentiary Commissioners and Sanger & Steele.

Q. State with whom the contract was made for the stone for the two next stories.

A. With Walker, of Lemont.

Q. Who was that contract made with?

A. With the Penitentiary Commissioners.

Q. What was your opinion, and advice to the State House Commissioners and the Penitentiary Commissioners, ae to which stone was the best suited for the work?

—19

A. My opinion was that the two lower foundation courses should be put in from the quarry of Sanger & Steele, because it was harder stone, and the quality in color would be compensated for by the hardness of the stone ; but that the balance of the stone for the basement story, to be taken from Sanger & Steele's quarry, would be objectionable, on account of the cost of cutting, for the moulding, &c.

Q. About what would be the difference in the cost of cutting the two kinds of stone : and which would cost the most ?

A. For mouldings, Sanger & Steele's stone would cost fifty per cent. the most, and in ordinary work about ten to fifteen per cent. the most.

Q. Will there be considerable moulding work ?

A. Yes, sir ; there is considerable moulding work upon the first story.

Q. Taking into consideration the cutting and preparing the stone for the building, which do you regard as the cheapest stone, Walker's at eighty cents, or the other at seventy-five cents.

A. Walker's would be the cheapest at $1.

Q. Do you know anything about the price of stone at the time that contract was made ?

A. Yes, sir.

Q. What was the price of stone of the character required for this building ?

A. In Chicago the price was from $1 00 to $1 20 per cubic foot—the large stone $1 20, and the thin stone $1 00 ; I don't think Sanger & Steele furnish much stone in Chicago ; the Illinois Stone Company and Walker was $1 10 upon an average per cubic foot.

Q. Do you know the object of the Penitentiary Commissioners was, and if they advised with us, what their object was in contracting at once for stone for the two next stories ?

A. Yes, sir ; Walker's stone is a very good, wide, even, clear stone, when selected, and can hardly be replaced by any other quarry ; and if the penitentiary commissioners contracted for one story alone, Walker could charge double price for the next story, the commissioners being unable to get stone from any other place.

Q. State if you gave it as your opinion that it was wise to make a contract for stone for both stories instead of one ?

A. Yes, sir; I gave it as my opinion that it was wise because if they contracted but for one story they would be under the contractors when it came to the next story.

Q. State whether you regard that as a good contract or a bad one for the State?

A. I regard that as a good contract for the State.

Q. Now I will get you to state how the size and thickness of the stone for the next story will compare with the stone in the basement story furnished by Sanger & Steele.

A. In the present basement story the stone in the base course is twenty-four inches. Most of the stone for the next story will be thicker. One course will be four feet, three inches and five-eighths; one four feet, three inches, etc. They are to lie upon a natural bed.

Q. What do you mean by a natural bed?

A. They are to be laid in the building the same as in the quarry, only dressed. Every stone is to lay in a natural bed, just as it laid in the quarry.

Q. You have seen Sanger & Steele's quarry?

A. Yes, sir.

Q. Could they furnish that stone?

A. No, sir.

Q. Have they any bed of stone of that thickness?

A. No, sir; they could not furnish the stone of the thickness required in the basement story.

Q. Do you know Mr. Garnsey, of Chicago?

A. Yes, sir.

Q. What is his character as an architect among professional men?

A. He is a young man, and I suppose he will be called a good architect if he lives long enough.

Q. Do you recollect what he said about what amount it would take, and what the cut stone would cost here two years ago?

A. He said the transportation of it alone would cost $340,000.

Q. What would the transportation actually cost?

A. From $95,000 to $100,000.

Q. In his statements there as to amounts, was there any reliability in them at all?

A. No, sir; no reliability whatever.

Q. Do you recollect what he said about what his opinion was at that time—at the time the plans were adopted—as to what the building would cost?

A. Yes, sir.

Q. What did he say in his testimony?

A. He said it would cost $5,000,000.

Q. Do you recollect whether he stated then that he had helped to make the plans and specifications which showed that it would cost less than $3,000,000?

A. Yes, sir, he did.

Q. Now, there has been a good deal said here about measurements. State anything you know about the measurement of the work.

A. I looked at Mr. Clark's measurements. I found one or two clerical errors in it—some favorable to him and some against the contractor. I found one instance in which Mr. Clark misunderstood the specification which amounted to some forty thousand brick, probably. It was a flue which I think was too large and ought to be counted like two walls. I think he misunderstands the specification.

Q. You understand the specification in that particular different from what he does?

A. Yes, sir. It is a flue, an air flue in the southwestern part of the dome. There may be some difficulty with reference to the air flue there. According to the specifications, I calculate it may be measured both ways, but according to fairness, I think ought to be measured full. But taking the legal view of it, I don't think I would measure it full. Some would measure it full and some would not. In fairness, I think it ought to be measured in full, but according to the specifications, I think it ought not to be. There are two arches there, one above the other, which I think ought to be measured solid.

Q. Now, speaking of these air flues or arches running clear through the building, from north to south—in the lower one of these there seems to be but little rise, what is the number of inches?

A. They are five and one-half inches or six inches. There are three of them, one after another.

Q. The one above has more spring?

A. Yes, sir.

Q. What weight is there upon the lower one?

A. No weight at all, except its own.

Q. Is that only one thickness of brick?

A. Yes, sir. Four inches in thickness, except the building of the haunches.

Q. There is no weight upon it, except the brick and mortar itself?

A. That is all.

Q. Is there any danger of their falling down?

A. No, sir.

Q. There are but very few brick in them?

A. There is no weight to it. I can make an arch as flat as that, that will bear as large a weight as any other.

Q. Is it not impossible for an arch to fall, unless the brick is crushed?

A. That is it; unless there is weight enough to crush the brick, it will not fall.

Q. If that arch should fall, would it injure the building?

A. No, sir. It would not hurt it a particle.

Q. Do you know Mr. Bollin-Stark?

A. Yes, sir. I know of him.

Q. Do you know anything of his capacity as an architect or engineer?

A. He worked for me last summer about a month, drawing a draught of a church in Keokuk, and I got him to do some work on the plans of the State House very well, to my satisfaction. He drew the perspective very well. He was pretty slow, and I could not keep him at the price I paid him, and discharged him.

Q. What is your opinion as to his capacity as an architect?

A. At the time I got him, I thought him a very fair draughtsman, but a little slow. When he quit me, I believe he said he wanted to go to Chicago, and wanted me to give him a recommendation, so that he could find employment. I wrote a recommendation, stating that what he did for me when in my employ, was done to my satisfaction. I never paid much attention to him since, except within the last five or six weeks.

Q. Do you know anything about his capacity as an engineer to measure work?

A. I have talked to the man since he was appointed to measure this work, and my candid opinion is that he cannot multiply one number of feet and inches by another number of feet and inches. That is, he can't multiply five feet five inches, by seven feet seven inches.

Q. Do you know how long he was in measuring that work, from any conversation you had with him?

A. I speak from observation. He was there a number of times. He was in my office sixteen or seventeen times during the time, remaining from five to ten minutes at a time.

Q. Have you ever had any conversation with him about his measurement?

A. Yes, sir. Once or twice, but he never told me himself how much he found or how much he measured it. He asked me if the arches were to be counted full. I told him yes. He asked me if the hall walls were to be counted full. I told him it was to be counted full.

Q. You know something of the capacity of Mr. Bolin-Starck and Garnsey, of Chicago, to measure work; and also of the capacity of Mr. Clark, the elder, as well as his son, for measuring work and making calculations?

A. Yes, sir.

Q. What is young Mr. Clark's capacity for measuring work?

A. He is pretty correct measurer.

Q. How is the old gentleman?

A. He is also correct.

Q. Now take the two measurements, that done by young Mr. Clark and that done by Bolin-Starck and Garnsey, which would you have the most faith in—Clark having the facilities for measuring, having seen the walls laid up?

A. I would have most faith in Mr. Clark's measurement.

Q. Is it your judgment that the measurement of Clark is correct?

A. It is substantially correct, except in the point I specified, where we understand the specifications differently.

Q. Which would make a difference of about forty thousand brick?

A. Yes, sir.

Q. Is there anything else you wish to speak about?

A. I think I can speak of the time it would take to measure such a building as that, in its present condition. A man who is not acquainted with the plans could not measure that building in less than a full week.

Q. How long was Garnsey here?

A. He told me he arrived on Saturday, and left on Monday night.

Q. Have you any means of knowing what time he spent upon the work?

A. I saw him on Saturday in the House of Representatives; except a little time in the morning, he was upon the ground. I saw him the whole of the afternoon, until five o'clock. On Sunday morning he didn't go to the building, because I was there myself a part of the time, and my boys were there a part of the time. Sunday afternoon he took some measurements.

Q. From the time he was there, and from his familiarity with the plans, could any reliance whatever be placed upon his judgment in that measurement?

A. No, sir.

Examination by Mr. Roberts, on behalf of the Committee:

Q. Where did you say you worked at architecture before you worked here?

A. I worked two years in Chicago, and since 1856 in St. Louis.

Q. What buildings erected in Chicago under your superintendence, or of which you are architect, in Chicago or other places?

A. We built some stores upon Wabash Avenue. We built the Bloomington Court House. I was in parnership with Mr. Cochrane, in Chicago.

Q. Was that after Mr. Cochrane was in partnership with Mr. Garnsey?

A. Yes, sir.

Q. You formed a partnership since he got the contract for the new State House?

A. Yes, sir.

Q. What buildings did you erect in St. Louis?

A. I could pick you out a good many in my office. I was the chief in the office of Mr. Walsh for two years. I was his foreman in building the Lindell Hotel. Mr. Walsh erected that building.

Q. Did you draw the plan and specifications of that hotel?

A. I made all the drawings for it, but not the specifications.

Q. How long have you been in partnership with Mr. Cochrane?

A. Since the fifth of February, 1868.

Q. How old a man is Mr. Cochrane?

A. He is thirty-eight years old, I think.

Q. How much older than Mr. Garnsey?

A. About ten years older. Mr recollection is, Mr. Garnsey said he was twenty-seven years old, two years ago.

Q. You think he is not much of an architect?

A. I have nothing to say against Mr. Garnsey.

Q. Do you know whether Mr. Wheelock is a good architect?

A. I have only been in Chicago two years, and cannot tell of his ability as an architect. I have heard some speak very favorably of him, and some speak very badly of him.

Q. What is the reputation of Mr. Boynton as an architect?

A. He has a pretty fair reputation.

Q. How with Mr. Lowring?

A. He has been out of the profession for two years, I think. I never saw Mr. Lowring but twice, I think, in my life.

Q. As to Mr. Bolin-Starck, you think he is not competent to measure?

A. Not to measure that work.

Q. You are satisfied of that from conversations with him?

A. Yes, sir, talking with him and asking a few questions.

Q. Do you know how long he was engaged in measuring that work?

A. No, sir, not exactly. I think I saw him there the first or second day after he commenced, and quite often since.

Q. Don't you know how he was engaged there the best part of two weeks?

A. No, sir, I know nothing about that.

Q. Didn't he have the plans. Didn't he get an order for them?

A. He had the plans.

Q. He had the plans to go by?

A. Yes, sir, but I never saw a building measured by plans when the building was up; that is neither professional nor customary. The proper way is to measure by the building, and not by the plans. You take the plans to aid you in marking the walls.

Q. Did he take the plans to aid him in measuring and marking the walls ?

A. He had the plans to mark the walls. I furnished him a drawing of the plans from which he could mark the walls. If he measured it as he ought to have done he must have every cubic foot in each wall, and should have compared his measurements with Clark's, and find out where the difference was, if there was any difference.

Q. You are satisfied that the measurement of young Clark is all right ?

A. Yes, sir.

Q. You are satisfied there is a difference only of about forty thousand brick ?

A. Yes, sir.

Q. Are the air flues to be measured solid or open ?

A. The specifications say the hall walls and smoke flues are to be measured solid.

Q. What salary do you and Mr. Cochrane get for superintending the construction of this State House ?

A. We get two and a half per cent. upon the cost of the building.

Q. How much of your time does it occupy ?

A. It occupies considerable of my time. Often all the time for a month. Sometimes I have a month or so when I don't have much to do.

Q. How often do you visit the building ?

A. Since I have lived in Springfield, except a few days, I was upon the grounds every day.

Q. How long would you stay upon the grounds ?

A. A half an hour or so.

Q. How do you occupy the rest of your time ?

A. In making drawings, etc.

Q. How much time does Mr. Cochrane give to it.

A. Part of his time.

Q. How much time does he spend on the grounds ?

A. When I am here it is not necessary for him to be on the grounds. He has been here a few times since I have been here, to see how things were going on.

Q. He is engaged in building other buildings all the time.

—20

A. Yes, sir.

Q. Have you been engaged in superintending other buildings since you have been here?

A. Yes, sir. A few buildings in Bloomington. We have also made the plans for the Iowa State House.

Q. Did you make the plans for the Iowa State House?

A. Yes, sir.

Q. Were they accepted?

A. Yes, sir.

Q. When?

A. I think it was in September of last year. I cannot give you the exact time.

Q. Are you superintending the building of that?

A. We will be when we get fairly started.

Q. You have the contract for superintending the building of that?

A. Yes, sir, we are the architects of it.

Q. Can you give the proper attention to this while superintending that?

A. Yes, sir, we can.

Q. What is that building to cost?

A. It is to cost $1,500,000, without the dome.

Q. You think this building can be finished for less than $3,000,000 according to the plans and specifications?

A. I think when that building is completed, the whole cost will come within the constitutional limit of the three millions and a half. I give that as a calculation I have made, and not as a guess. It is an exact calculation of the cost of the work and materials.

Q. Has that building not cost more than the original calculation, already.

A. If the original calculation is that of two years ago, I say it was done for less.

Q. The calculation of four years ago.

A. I had nothing to do with the calculation of four years ago.

Q. Who made the first calculation?

A. I suppose Messrs. Cochrare & Garnsey.

Q. Don't you know the building has cost more than that first calculation? Nearly double as much.

A. I know it has cost more; if a man makes an estimate without knowing the ground upon which the building is to stand, it is not likely to be correct; if that building was erected on a natural bed of rock, three or four feet thick, or a bed of hard clay, four or five feet thick, it could have been built at the first estimate.

Examination resumed—by Mr. Robinson:

Q. You were not with Mr. Cochrane when that foundation was laid?

A, No, sir.

Q. The reason why it cost more than the estimate, was because they had to go down deeper for a solid foundation.

A. Yes, sir.

Q. Has the work that has been done since your estimate was made, and the estimate of the two Chicago architects, cost more or less than those estimates?

A. It has cost less than those estimates.

Q. What is the usual per cent. in this country, received by architects for making plans and specifications of buildings, and superintending the work?

A. They get five per cent.; I must add that in St. Louis they diminish only one per cent. for ever $500,000 after the first $500,000.

Q. What per cent. do you get upon the Iowa State House?

A. That is not definitely settled yet; they pay us for our expenses and time for the first year.

Q What per cent. did you get upon the Bloomington Court House?

A. We got five per cent.

Q. I want to call your attention to one other thing; I want you to name a few of the prominent buildings in this country and Europe, and state what was paid for the plans;

A. There has never been in this country, except in Washington, any building erected that compares with this new State House in size and cost; I know Mr. Barry got five per cent. for the new House of Parliament.

Q. I am speaking now of the plans.

A. For the plans and specifications two and a half per cent.

Q. Was $3,000 for the plans of this new State House an unreasonable amount?

A. No, sir; I considered it very cheap, and if it had not been for the honor of building such a house, I don't think there would have been any competition.

Q. Is it customary for architects to have a number of buildings going on at the same time?

A. It is common and usual.

Q. About what number of men do you keep employed all the time in the office keeping the plans up?.

A. I have had as high as twelve men employed upon this building. I have now four men. Sometimes I have three, four or five—depends upon how the work is going on. Upon an average we have certainly had four men employed all the time since we started. For months we had as high as twelve.

Q. You may state if it is true that about two years ago you were required by the Commissioners to make full and complete plans and specifications of the building, for the purpose of, under the law, of furnishing them to the Penitentiary Commissioners, and to two or three Committees of the House, to be passed upon?

A. Yes, sir.

Q. Did you go to work and make those plans and specifications?

A. I did.

Q. About how long were you at work at them?

A. I could not exactly remember the number of days. I think some seven or eight weeks. We had thirteen or fourteen men employed. We got all the men we could in Chicago.

Q. Were they the same plans that were submitted to those two architects and master builder of Chicago?

A. Yes, sir.

Q. What did they do with those plans? Did they make new plans or go over your's and see that they were right?

A. They went over my plans to see if they were right, and to see if the price we set upon the work was correct. They made new estimates of the work upon the plans we furnished them, but they didn't make a set of new plans.

Q. Are these plans any advantage to you in the progress of the work?

A. Not much.

Q. Do you have all your plans to make over by sections?

A. Yes, sir. The plans have all to be made over.

Q. What did you get for making those plans for those architects?

A. I got $5,000.

Q. Were you well satisfied with that?

A. No, sir. We asked ten thousand dollars. We thought five thousand was too little. I gave about two months of my time, day and night to the work. I thought if I could not make a thousand dollars a month at that kind of work, working day and night, it was pretty cheap. After we paid our hands we didn't have much left.

Re-Examination by Mr. Roberts, on behalf of the Committee:

Q. What do these hands do whom you keep in your employ?

A. They work in the drawings after I pencil them out; occupied in tracing, and so forth. The best thing for you to do is to go to the office and see what they are doing. They are making plans for each stone in the building. Each separate stone has to be marked out; a drawing has to be made of every stone, one above another. The size, length and height, with every jog, and every piece has to be marked out, so the stone cutter cannot possibly mistake one stone for another. There is not one stone in that building that is not drawn five times.

Q. Then you think when you are at work at that kind of business, your services are worth $1,000 a month.

A. Yes, sir. When I work day and night. I didn't sleep more than four hours any night while I was making those drawings.

Q. The Commissioners gave you five thousand dollars for drawing those duplicate plans?

A. Yes, sir.

Wm. Clark, sworn.

Direct—by Mr. Robinson, Commissioner:

Q State if you have been employed on the new State House?

A. Yes, sir; I have.

Q. How long?

A. Well, it will be two years next July since I came there.

Q. What have you been engaged in?

A. When I first came there I helped to lay out work on the walls and foundations ; this year I measured the stone and brick work.

Q. This year ?

A. I mean last year.

Q. What portion of the brick work did you measure ?

A. Well, I measured the whole of the new walls.

Q. Explain how you measured it ?

A. I measured every month as they went along ; and when the walls were completed, I measured it over again. I measured the courses of stone as they were laid, and the courses of brick.

Q. Have you kept the figures of your measurement ?

A. Yes, sir.

Q. Where are they ?

A. Keep them in that book. (Pointing.)

Q. What does that show ?

A. Hight, length, thickness ; in every wall by itself.

Q. Is it made in sections ?

A. I drew a plan of the basement.

Q. Take the paper and explain ?

A. (Witness explains the plan.) I measured from the spring of the arch. (Witness explains one as follows:) One opening is eleven feet two inches wide, thirteen feet six inches high, one brick wide and sixty-five one hundredths, which makes the total ninety-nine; so on all the way down.

Q. Can any person who is qualified take this book and the plans in the office, and tell whether they are correct or not ?

A. They can take this book with a tapeline and go right out on the walls and tell ; of course I measured them from the walls.

Q. You say an engineer that is qualified can take this book and measure the work correctly ?

A. Yes, sir ; the inside walls. The outside walls I don't think he could.

Q. Then, if there is any error in your measurement, can a man take your book and detect it ?

A. Yes, sir ; by going out on the walls and measuring.

Q. Are these your figures—is this a copy of that ?

A. Yes, sir ; I suppose it is. These here I kept myself.

Q. In your judgment, is your measurement correct ?

A. Yes, sir.

Q. Who directed you to measure ?

A. My father.

Q. Your father is Assistant Superintendent ?

A. Yes, sir.

Q. Did your father give you any directions about measuring ?

A. Yes, sir.

Q. If there is any mistake at all, it is in the adding ?

A. Yes, sir; although in the outside walls there may be a portion of the width and length ; yet it all comes out right in the end.

Q. As I understand, at the end of each month you measured ; what for ?

A. For monthly estimates.

Q. Did you keep that measurement ?

A. Yes, sir.

Q. When the work was entirely finished, did you go over and measure again ?

A. When it was finished, I measured up again.

Q. In your judgment, how much time did you spend ?

A. When I commenced this book it took me about two weeks, but for monthly estimates, it took me about three days.

Q. Did your father give you any caution about being careful ?

A. Yes, sir, he did so.

Q. If there is any mistake, then, you don't know it ?

A. No sir, I do not.

Q. You were directed to do it correctly, and you did ?

A. Yes, sir.

By Mr. McMillan.

Q. Did you take any pains to verify your work—prove it ?

A. Yes, sir.

Q. Did you measure it over again ?

A. Yes, sir.

By Mr. Robinson, Commissioner.

Q. You will describe how much care you took ?

A. Well. I took all the care I could. I measured it over two or three times, and figured it three or four times.

Q. Are the arches in the sub-basement all the same hight from the spring to the floor, or do they differ ?

A. They differ [looking at his book] two or three-tenths. Here is one differs five-tenths of a foot.

Cross Examination—by Mr. Robinson.

Q. How old are you?
A. Nineteen last March.
Q. Your father is assistant superintendent?
A. Yes, sir.
Q. For whom were you at work?
A. The Commissioners.
Q. What is your business?
A. My business the first year was to assist in laying out the walls.
Q. How old were you then?
A. Sixteen.
Q. What have you been doing since?
A. I have been measuring the stone, helping to lay out the work and looking up for estimates.
Q. Are you competent to measure things of that kind?
A. Yes, sir.
Q. Made it your study?
A. Yes, sir, with the knowledge my father has given me.
Q. Where did you study?
A. Practiced with him.
Q. Ever engaged before in this work?
A. Yes, sir, in Davenport.
Q. What were you doing there?
A. Father was engineer. I did a good deal of work.
Q. Before you were sixteen years old?
A. Yes, sir.
Q. Been in the habit of measuring brick in walls?
A. With my father.
Q. Not without him?
A. Yes, sir.
Q. Was it all correct?
A. Yes, sir, so far as I know.
Q. Under whose directions did you do this?
A. My father's.
Q Did you have anybody to assist you?
A. Yes, sir, Sam Downing.
Q. Who is he? Where does he live?

A. Don't know where he is now. Went from here up north; had him hold the tape line for me.

Q. Was that during the whole time? How much did he help you?

A. Mr. Robinson's son helped the first part of the season.

Q. You're satisfied your figures are correct?

A. Yes, sir.

Q. Entirely in accordance with the specifications?

A. Yes, sir, under father's advice.

Q. Who was paying you?

A. The Commissioners—$90 00 a month.

Q. When did you first commence measuring?

A. Well, I don't remember when. I think it was in May, last year.

Q. Did you measure the brick in the cellar?

A. Yes, sir.

Q. That had been laid before you measured any? When was the last brick in the cellar laid?

A. Don't remember, sir.

Q. You measured it as it was laid, did you?

A. Yes, sir.

Q. Was your father always present when you were measuring?

A. Always on the building.

Q. Who helped you to make up the figures?

A. This young Mr. Downing.

Q. When was that?

A. This last February.

Q. You figured it all up to that time?

A. Yes, sir; that finished the contract.

Q. How many bricks did you return to the Commissioners as laid in the walls?

A. 7,514,745 85-100.

Re direct—by Mr. Robinson, *Commissioner.*

Q. Did your father superintend your measuring and your figuring?

A. Yes, sir.

Q. Did he do that carefully and closely?

A. He used to advise me a good deal about it.

Q. Watch the whole thing?

—21

A. Yes, sir.

Q. A person can take your books and go over the plans of the building, and see whether you've made mistakes or not?

A. Yes, sir; he can go right out on the walls and measure the arches and inside walls, but the outside walls I don't think he could.

Q. Were you out the other evening with Richardson, Sherman and others, in measuring some work?

A. Yes, sir.

Q. What was their manner of measurement?

A. They said if they were going to measure they would measure right around the corners; that wasn't the way I did.

Q. How do their figures agree with yours?

A. Within a fraction; when I measured there was a good deal of rubbish and one thing or another around there; I couldn't make it exact.

Q. Every month you would show how many brick had been laid for the purpose of monthly estimates? and that was all recorded?

A. Yes, sir.

Q. You spoke of measuring according to specifications—did your father tell you what the specifications said, and advise you?

A. Yes, sir; I worked according to his directions.

By Mr. McMillan:

Q. Conceding that your measurement of the hight, thickness and length of the walls is correct, as stated in your book, can the measurement of the quantity of brick be approved by an examination of your book?

A. Yes sir.

—

David Sherman, sworn.

Direct Examination, by Mr. Robinson, *Commissioner:*

Q. Where do you reside?

A. In Springfield.

Q. How long have you lived here?

A. Thirty-two years.

Q. What have you been engaged in?

A. The early part of my life a builder, afterward a contractor, and for several years connected with the Illinois Central and other railroads. On the Illinois Central I was agent for purchasing, and engaged in constructing, superintending and building culverts, tank houses, etc. On this road I was the purchasing agent—that means, purchasing any articles wanted for machinery, lumber, ties, timber, and everything of that kind; purchasing for machinery comes under the head of master mechanic, but almost everything else outside is a department. For instance, there is the ticket agent; he has the purchasing of his coupons. I only state this that you may know there are different departments as purchasing agent.

Q. During the time you were connected with the Central road had you an opportunity, or was it your duty, to notice, among other things, brick work?

A. Yes, sir; I had a good deal of that in the way of culverts, arches—small culverts built of brick.

Q. Do you regard yourself a judge of brick masonry?

A. Yes, sir; I have an opinion that I understand it.

Q. What opportunity have you had to examine the work on the new State House during its progress?

A. Well, I, as a citizen of Springfield, and of the State of Illinois, have always felt an interest in public improvements. I live about 150 or 200 feet southwest of the State House grounds, and going to the city I passed through the grounds almost every day; and being in no particular business I have frequently stopped and watched the progress of the workmen, to see how they were progressing; and in my judgment I think the work is as well done as ever I saw on any public structure.

Q. Have you examined it since the work has ceased, particularly?

A. I was called upon by the Commissioners to take the plans and measurement, in company with other gentlemen, and see whether there were any defects in the measurement. We did so, and I had the plan before me, and the plan has different sections. I haven't it with me now; some one has it. In section sixteen, Mr. Clark's son had measured the work. We found the hight of the walls to be nineteen feet and five inches; referring to the book we found that Mr. Clark had made it nineteen feet three inches, giving to the State the benefit of two inches on the wall; and taking other sections together with section sixteen, supposing them to correspond with what we measured, there would be considerable benefit to the State; and were I the contractor, knowing this, I should rather the walls were measured over again.

Q. Did you make any further measurements in any other part of the building?

A. We measured some of the arches to see whether the openings were measured correctly; but in doing so I found all correct; at least, so far as the spring of the arch to the crown of the arch is concerned. It has always been customary, in my experience, to measure that way. It has become a custom in this country to measure in the culverts of a building, or anything else.

Q. Did you have with you the specifications for this brick work?

A. Yes, sir; one of us carried it—Mr. Richardson, I think—and read it over as we called on him.

Q. So far as you know, were the measurements made in accordance with them?

A. I thought so.

Q. Your opinion was, if you were the contractor, you would prefer to have the work re-measured.

A. I certainly would, sir.

Q. Did you examine the holes? Do you know where they are located.

A. One is located on the southeast portion of the building, and the other, I should judge, a little west, on the opposite side of the corridor, in the southwest portion of the building.

Q. Did you examine the mortar and the brick work?

A. We did so. We were there some time, and expressed our opinion about it.

Q. Did you notice the manner of laying the brick, whether they were wet and well imbedded in the mortar?

A. The brick were wet before they went into the wall. For instance, they would bring their hose to bear on a pile of brick so as to wet them sufficiently, then they were taken out and they were laid in the mortar. If laid without wetting, the mortar generally adheres to the brick right away, the brick absorbs all the moisture of the mortar, and sometimes doesn't make a good piece of work.

Q. Did you notice the grouting?

A. Yes, sir. Above and in the cellar. I thought they put in more grouting than was necessary, because I noticed in tying the walls together—every third course, I think, is tied. We don't generally tie more than once in about nine courses. The grouting was made there and poured down, so as to fill up all the crevices between the brick.

Q. Have you had considerable talk with young Clark, so as to satisfy you of his capacity and ability?

A. More in the last five or six weeks, probably, than heretofore, as I have been somewhat connected with him in the measuring of the work. I find that he is a very correct young man, and and I should be willing, if I was in business, to trust to his judgment in measuring any jobs of work, where the work is all square.

Q. Do you know anything about the capacity of his father?

A. No, sir.

Cross-Examination by Mr. ROBERTS:

Q. What is your business now?

A. I am in no particular business.

Q. Have you been engaged in building, brick building?

A. I was in the early part of my life.

Q. How long is it since you finished?

A. In 1854 I think was the last.

Q. Have you examined the sand out of which this mortar is made?

A. I have known of it for forty years. We have used it for all our building—river sand and bluff.

Q. Which is the best?

A. I don't know that I would have a choice in cementing cisterns. I have frequently bought the river sand, being told it was better to make plaster, but for laying brick I should prefer the other.

Q. Have you examined these walls this spring?

A. Yes, sir.

Q. Did you find the mortar well set?

A. Yes, sir. As well as under the same circumstances any wall of the same thickness would be. A wall two feet, three or four feet, cannot dry through for a long time—some say a year—especially where the brick were well wet.

Q. Do you think the mortar is as well set as it could be under the circumstances.

A. I think so, and last winter if they had covered the walls probably they might have saved two or three courses of brick—that's all.

Q. Did you notice the openings, windows and doors—whether two or three courses had been injured there?

A. Two or three courses may be in the openings in the main passage.

Q. The windows, the openings in the interior walls—did you notice were they injured?

A. No more than would naturally be the effect of bad weather.

Q. Do you think they would be as much effected as the walls on top?

A. They would certainly, if the exposure were equal.

Q. Where there is a wall above them?

A. Perhaps not, if we could expect the rain always to fall straight down and the weather always to freeze perpendicularly.

Q. Do you think they are just as much exposed as the wall on top?

A. I think so.

Q. Do you think this lime and sand would make good mortar?

A. I think so—either the bluff sand or the other. I noticed the bluff and river sand together; some mix. I am told by men who are still building here they prefer it so.

Q. Do you know anything about the kind of lime they use?

A. I do not, sir. Only as I saw it made in mortar.

Re-direct Examination—By Mr. Robinson, Commissioner.

Q. Would taking off two or three courses be more expensive? Wouldn't it cost as much to have covered the building?

A. I suppose it would more, and then perhaps it wouldn't have had the desired effect, for the walls were laid late in the season, and they wouldn't have dried enough to be protected.

William Shepherd sworn.

Direct—By Mr. Robinson, Commissioner:

Q. What is your name?

A. Wm. Shepherd.

Q. Where do you reside?

A. In Jerseyville, Jersey county, in this State.

Q. What has been your business?

A. Well, I have been engaged in different businesses—railroad, canal, etc.

Q. What I want to get at is this: How much experience have you had in brick masonry and stone, so as to be a competent judge of that kind of work.

A. I have considerable to do with masonry in railroad bridges —with brick work not so much as with stone. I have built some brick buildings of my own as well as brick bridges.

Q. Are you a judge of the stability of work?

A. I do not claim to be an expert. I have a great deal to do with work—not so much in buildings as in bridges. I claim to myself to have some little idea of brick work, but I do not set myself down here as an expert.

Q. I will get you to state whether you have examined the work of this new State House, and if so, at what different times?

A. I examined it last fall. I was at Springfield, and out of curiosity went over and looked at the State House. I have examined it twice since. I haven't gone into a critical examination like experts, merely a general view.

Q. What is your judgment of the brick work?

A. There is no question about it in my opinion. It is a good piece of work—unusually so. I must explain: there I could find brick work there that is very inferior, to look at it. Take, for instance, that brick wall on top; but the brick work that hasn't been affected by the frost is good. The tops of all buildings, in my observation, when exposed to the weather are affected so that they have to be torn down. I was unfortunate once to have six feet tore down; still, I think that was bad workmanship. But one or two feet on the top of this wall would be necessary to tear down. With that exception, I consider the whole a fine piece of work.

Q. You're one of the Senate Committee on Public Buildings who had to examine the plans and specifications of this building?

A. Yes, sir.

Q. Did you give it strict attention?

A. Yes, sir. I was one of the committee with Carter, Bauer, master builder, Deikman.

Q. What were they employed for?

A. In the first place, to help the committee make their report as to the cost. A very serious question was as to the cost Another serious question was as to the plans of Mr. Cochrane, whether or not they would make a good respectable building and one that would be a credit to the state. The committee met in Joliet—a joint committee of the two houses—and I believe all the business they did was to appoint a special committee, with authority to employ two architects and a master builder, to examine the plans and specifications as submitted by Mr. Cochrane, to see whether these plans would make a suitable building.

Q. State if you employed them?

A. General Fuller, Munsen, Baker, Cook, of Lake, and myself. We employed those architects. They went to work on the plans submitted by Mr. Cochrane. Their attention was called to the point, to figure out the actual cost of this building. Another point was as to the character of the building—its permanency. They went to work, those gentlemen, and spent, I should say, two or three months. From the plans of Mr. Cochrane they made a detailed statement of the entire cost of the building. We sent them to New York, Philadelphia and different shops to get the prices of different kind of materials, they basing their estimates upon their own information obtained in this way, and upon their own skill and knowledge as architects. I might say every stone was figured on, every brick and every piece of wood or iron that entered into the building; and the most thorough examination of the plans was made and filed. You will find in that report, if I am not mistaken, a detailed estimate of everything that enters into the building. They made some changes, in the way of suggestions, which were adopted by the committee.

By Mr. ROBERTS:

Q. That report was printed?

A. I think it was. If my recollection serves me right, they figured out the cost of that building about $3,000,000, including all that had been done. I am speaking generally. I had forgotten what the increase was on account of the changes. The object was to make it as near fire-proof as possible.

Q. I think there is an estimate of the number of brick for each story?

A. In my recollection, there is; but I speak guardedly, for I cannot say, positively.

By Mr. ROBINSON:

Q. Did you, when selecting those men, endeavor to select men of good character in their profession at Chicago?

A. It was an important question to get proper architects. We wanted to get a capable gentleman. Our first impression was to go to Philadelphia or St. Louis. We discussed the question thoroughly. Finally, we made a contract with Mr. Bauer and Mr.

Carter. Each one of our committee was to make particular enquiries concerning those gentlemen. I know I made it my business, among my business acquaintances in Chicago, (and I have a large number of acquaintances there)—I made it my business to inquire as to the standing of those architects. Mr. Fuller, who was on the committee with me, also inquired very particularly amongst his friends, until finally we came to the conclusion that they were gentlemen fully confident and entirely reliable. And I would add here, at this time, what I have heard of them since. I wouldn't hesitate to say I consider them two as reliable gentlemen as you will find in the United States of America; and Mr. Bauer—though I do not mean to disparage Mr. Carter—I consider more than ordinary in his profession.

Q. Do you recollect what their charge was?

A. About $13,000.

Q. State whether your committee recommended the payment of that amount?

A. We did, sir. My opinion was, it was a pretty heavy charge, but I knew it had taken them from their office, and I knew the time it had required. I think they paid about $1,000 for employees; and while it seemed to me a large charge, I may say, all things considered, I was prepared to vote for it, and am prepared to vote for it now.

Q. They made their report back to your sub-committee and you reported back to the joint committee. Then passed the two houses an order to the commissioners to proceed with the work?

A. Yes, sir, the sub-committee was authorized, when they were ready to report, to call the joint committee, and the joint committee authorized them to fix the time, which was done by General Fuller. They met here at Springfield, and the report of the architect was approved, together with their bill of thirteen thousand dollars, and the commissioners were authorized to proceed.

Q. What is your recollection as to the plans of Mr. Cochrane?

A. I think there was some changes which increased the cost.

Q. Mr. Piquenard says about eighty-five thousand dollars.

A. My recollection is that is about right.

Q. From the reputation of those architects and your general knowledge of work, will you let me ask you if you would be willing to contract to build that building according to the plans and specifications inside of the amount of money named in the Constition?

A. Yes, sir. I should be willing to build that building according to the plans as changed to some extent and approved by the committee, for three million of dollars, or, I should say, three and a quarter. I should want a quarter to go on, though. I should not hesitate to do it for three million, and if the committee will bear with me, I will explain why I would do it.

Mr. Roberts:

Go ahead.

A. In the first place, as I said before, I have such confidence in these two architects and the master builder, (I don't claim myself to be an adept) and in the care with which they investigated this matter, and the confidence I have in the judgment of these two gentlemen, as well as some little knowledge of my own in brick work and masonry, I would not hesitate at all to take it at that price. Materials of the same kind are cheaper now than they were then. I have some little property which I would be willing to risk, and I should feel as certain as of any contract I ever took in my life.

Q. You are willing to enter into bonds and take it?

A. Yes. I don't think it is a question—you will excuse me, Mr. Chairman, for speaking so freely—I don't think it is a question that needs discussion, and you will excuse me again; the reporter need not put this down.

Mr. Roberts:

Oh, go on; say what you please.

A. I was going to say I have no patience with the discussion; this State House report to which I refer was not got up as an ordinary estimate; the entire credit of those architects there was at stake—a point which they well understood, and their investigation was made with more than ordinary care.

Mr. Robinson, Commissioner:

Do you wish to examine him, Mr. Roberts?

Mr. Roberts:

No; I don't want to ask him anything.

F. H. Piquenard—recalled.

Direct—by Mr. Robinson, Commissioner:

Q. I want to ask you a general question. Do you regard this brick masonry as good work?

A. Yes, sir.

Q. Do you regard those walls as perfectly sound?

A. Yes, sir.

Q. Did you pay any attention to this mortar as it was being made?

A. Yes, sir.

Q. State whether the mortar was good, and whether this sand-lime there used was calculated to make good mortar?

A. Yes, sir; the mortar will become very hard, and so much the harder because of a longer time to dry; and as I don't want any body to rely upon my judgment alone, I have brought a few authorities with me.

[The witness here read from page 99, of Lefevre, also, from a work by Mahone, late Professor of Engineering at West Point. The Committee decided that he might have leave to furnish the reporter with copies of the extracts—and accordingly the reporter has been provided with the following:]

The mortar we used is a slightly or moderately hydraulic mortar, which will continue to harden perceptibly for at least three years, when under water or in dampness.

On account of the heavy thickness of our walls, of the wetting of the bricks, and of grouting every course, added to the wet weather of the last fall and winter, our walls have been kept as damp as possible, and have not dried yet, which we consider an immense advantage, as our mortar will have had time to perfect its full chemical reaction and crystalization before it is fully dry.

In support of my views, I give hereinafter a few American authorities on the subjert, leaving aside any French, English, or German authorities which came to the same conclusion:

Gen. Gillmore, in his practical treatise on limes, hydraulic cements and mortar, Ed. 1864, says:

Art. 331. A paste of the hydrate of fat lime, in free contact with the atmosphere, absorbs carbonic acid gas upon the surface, although not to the point of saturnation, and becomes coated with a mixture of hydrate and carbonate of lime (Ca. O. C. O. 2, x Ca. O. H. O.), the gas gradually penetrates the substance at a rate of progress constantly on the decrease, and at the end of one year, according to Mr. Nicat, the layer of impure carbonate is from 10 to 12 hundredths part of an inch in depth.

Art. 332. The incrustation is due in the case of hydraulic limes to the combined influence of reactions, considerably more complicated and obscure. Hydrosilicate and aluminate of lime (Si. O's x Ca. O. x 6. H. O., and Al. 2, O. 2 x 3, Ca. O. x 6 H. O.) are found in addition to the hydro carbonate. The formation of these compounds is not confined to the crust on the surface, but takes places throughout the mass, and is really the principal efficient cause of the induration of this class of lime.

Art. 581. Mortar of common lime becomes sufficiently strong to resist a powerful force of compression long before they exhibit any adhesion to the solid materials. *Such mortars obtain their maximum strength and hardness only after the lapse of years*, and even *centuries.*

Our lime being slightly hydraulic, will take but a few years to do the same effect.

From D. H. Mahan, "*Course of Civil Engineering*," for the use of the cadets of the U. S. Military Academy, we find in the following paragraphs :

SEC 42. Some of the hydraulic limes harden, or set, *very slowly* under water, while others set rapidly.

SEC. 78. Dry hydrates of limes converted into a thick paste and exposed to the air, gradually absord carbonic acid. This action first takes place on the surface, and *proceeds more slowly from year to year* towards the interior of the exposed mass. The absorption proceeds more rapidly in the meagre or hydraulic limes than in the fat limes.

SEC. 114. Any pure sand, mixed in proper proportions with hydraulic lime, will give a good mortar for the open air; fine sand yields the best mortar with good hydraulic lime; mixed sand with the feebly hydraulic limes, and course sand with fat lime.

SEC. 124. The quick-setting hydraulic limes are said to furnish a mortar which, in time, acquires neither as much strength or hardness as that from the slower setting hydraulic limes.

SEC. 125. Mortars of strong hydraulic limes placed in water (or kept damp) do not show any appreciable increase of hardness after the second year. Then how long will they show it, if only slightly hydraulic?

SEC. 126. The paste of a hydrate, either of common or hydraulic lime, when exposed to the air, absorbs carbonic acid gas from it, passes to the state of sub-carbonate of lime, without, however, rejecting the water of the hydrate, and *gradually hardens.*

The time required for the complete saturation of the mass exposed will depend on its bulk.

The absorption of the gas commences at the surface and *proceeds more slowly towards the center.*

139. The adhesion of common mortar to bricks and stone *for the first*

few years is greater than the cohesion of its own particles. The force with which hydraulic cement adheres to the same materials is less than the cohesion of its own particles.

292. From experiments made on small prisms *one year old.* (Being small they could harden all throughout.) Mr. Nicat found that the resistance of mortar to a transversal strain is for

Mortars of very strong	hydraulic	lime,..................	170 lbs.
" ordinary	"	"	140 "
" medium	"	"	100 "
" common lime	"	"	40 "
" bad quality	"	"	10 "

(The mortar made of the lime used in the State House, in one of the arches where the setting and hardening has been more easily done, that in the walls, though not as well as in very small·prisms, will give a resistance after ten months of over 70 lbs.)

365. The mortar bed of bricks may be either of ordinary, or thin tempered mortar, the last however is the best, as it makes closer joints, *and containing more water does not dry so rapidly as the other.*

As brick has greater avidity for water it would always be well not only to moisten it before laying it, but to allow it to soak in water several hours before it is used.

By taking this precaution, the mortar between the joints *will set more firmly* than when it imparts its water to the dry bricks, which it frequently does so rapidly as to render the mortar *pulverulent* when it has dried.

In a preceding paragraph, No. 53, after speaking of the way of making the experiments to test the qualities of lime in placing a lump of paste in a tumbler of water, he says: "If lime is only moderately hydraulic, it will have become hard enough at the end of fifteen or twenty days to resist the pressure of the finger, and will continue to *harden slowly*, more particularly from the six or eight months after immersion ; and at *the end of a year* it will have acquired the consistency of hard soap, and will dissolve slowly in pure water.

"It is the case with the lime we used in the work."

Mr. M. Lafever in his treatise on architecture, speaking of the theory of induration of mortar by crystalization from the surface to the center, adds : "That the crystalization may be more perfect, a large quantity of water should be used, the ingredients perfectly mixed together, *and the drying be as slow as possible.*

An attention to these particulars would make the buildings of the moderns equally durable with those of the ancients. *In the old Roman works, the great thickness of the walls necessarily required a vast length of time to dry.*"

Many other good authorities could be added, to prove that on account of the thickness of the walls in the State House, the mortar, could not dry and harden as fast as in lighter work; but that the mortar will be all the better for the slow operation. The preceding will be sufficient to prove our position before the committee.

[The witness, after reading, continued:]

A. I want to say right on, that this brick work is as good as can be found in this State or any other. I pretend to say [the witness herethen approached the brick wall of the church in which the investigation was held] if you cut inside of that, the mortar is pulverized—cut down an inch and it's pulverulent. It is not as good as our wall would be—it will never be as good as our wall—it dried too fast.

Q. Do you know how long Mr. Boyington was here two years ago?

A. He was here two days—perhaps three.

Q. Do you know whether that was a correct copy of his letter? Take these letters and look them over one by one.

A. This letter is from Mr. A. S. Andrews, in answer to a letter of mine; here is a letter from Addison Hutton; here is a letter from Mr. McArthur, also in answer to one of mine; here is a letter from Samuel Sloan, of Philadelphia, in answer to a letter of mine.

Q. Do you know these gentlemen to be architects?

A. Yes, sir; very well know Mr. Samuel Sloan is one of the oldest in the country, and Mr. McArthur also. This is one from Mr. Barker—Jessce—in answer to a letter of mine; here is a letter from Governor Geary--Governor of Pennsylvania—in answer to a letter of mine.

—

Richard P. Morgan, Jr., sworn and examined by Mr. Robinson, on behalf of the Commissioners—the members of the committee not being present.

Q. Where do you reside?

A. In Bloomington, Illinois.

Q. How long have you lived in this State?

A. Since 1852, about nineteen years.

Q. What has been your business?

A. I am following engineering. I might modify my first answer a little. I came to this State in 1847, and remained here three years. I was one year engaged upon the canal.

Q. Have you had any experience in building in brick masonry?

A. Yes, sir.

Q. To what extent? Go on and state what you have done and seen.

A. My experience commenced, practically, in 1847, upon the Illinois and Michigan Canal, upon the brick and stone work. I had the inspection of the stone and brick work of the locks. From thence I went on the Hudson River Railroad, in 1849, and was connected with that. I guess it was in 1848. I was connected with that during its entire construction, which involved almost every class of work in brick and stone, every character of brick arches, brick buildings, brick foundations, cut and rubble stone work, and every class of work nearly, and the use of cement and lime, etc.

Q. How recently have you been engaged in any building or overseering any building of any kind?

A. I have not had the immediate supervision of any building within four or five years, but as a matter of professional interest, I have examined almost all the leading buildings in the country.

Q. Name some of the most prominent you have examined.

A. The Patent Office at Washington, the new wings of the Capitol, the new Postoffice at Boston, and the Postoffice in Chicago, which is a very fine building; and several times when I have been at Springfield I have made examinations of the work upon the new State House here.

Q. I will now ask you the question if you have examined this work upon the new State House? If so, about how often have you seen it, and at what stages?

A. I saw it soon after the foundations were laid, and before they were up anywhere near completion. I have examined the building five times during the course of its construction—four or five times. I did so as a matter of professional interest, as I have, wherever I go, been in the habit of examining anything of that kind that is going on.

Q. How recently have you examined it?

A. The last examination I made was this afternoon. I went

over and saw part of the wall that was taken out. I examined it about a month ago also, or a little over a month ago.

Q. When you speak of a part of the wall taken out, do you mean that aperture taken out of the wall ?

A. Yes, sir.

Q. Does that enable you to get a good view, and so as to form a correct estimate of the class of work ?

A. Yes, sir, that certainly gives you a very good idea of the work.

Q. Will you now state what your judgment is as to that work on the new State House ?

A. My examination, as I stated before, has been only dictated by professional interest, and I may add to that the natural interest which a citizen of our State would take in the building. I have given it a careful examination several times. I regard the work as well adapted to the purpose, and well done. The walls are well lined, and has all the indications of being done in a substantial and mechanical manner.

Q. You regard it as perfectly safe to go on and complete the building upon those walls ?

A. Yes, sir, I have no doubt about it. The defects there are entirely superficial. The effect of the frost gives some parts there a rugged appearance about the surface, but does not in the slightest degree characterize the work or injure it substantially.

Q. Do you examine the mortar used in those walls ?

A. I directed my attention to every part of the work. I examine the cement always, as a matter of habit. I examined the mortar and everything else connected with it on each occasion.

Q. You regard it as a good job ?

A. Yes, sir.

Q. It is hardly worth while for me to ask you, but do you regard yourself as a competent judge of such work ?

A. My experience dates back to my childhood—my father has been an engineer all his life—and from the time I was able to understand anything, the leading topic in the house has been upon subjects of this character. I have had a personal experience of over twenty five years, so that perhaps I may, say I may claim to be competent to judge of such work.

Q. From the examination you have made of this work, how long, in your judgment, would it take an engineer, a man qualified for it, to measure all the work together upon that ground, and make a calculation so as to show correctly the number of brick in the building as it is to-day?

A. I don't know whether he could do it at all without considerable work to arrive at it, so as to make correct measurements. As I understand the work, he would have to open some parts of the building to disclose the work and get the measurement. I have not examined it particularly in respect to measuring, but naturally that would be a necessity.

Q. How long do you think it would take you, so that you would be willing to give an opinion, under oath, as to the number of brick, so as to be satisfactory to yourself to take the entire brick work?

A. That includes all the sub work.

Q. Yes, sir, entirely; all the brick work in the whole building?

A. I should think it might be done in from three days to a week. It would be attended with a good deal of difficulty. You may appriate the amount with less time and less labor, but as for what would be called a correct and final estimate, I think perhaps, it would require from three to six days to do it.

Q. Could that be done without either breaking part of the walls, or the stone on top of the arches?

A. No, sir. Unless the proportions were given to the party. If he was obliged to find them himself, he must separate, otherwise he could not testify to it. Of course, if the plans were given to a person, and he be requested to make the measurements from them it could be done in less time.

Q. What is the professional practice in measuring work after the work is done, measuring from the plans or measuring from the work itself?

A. You make your measurement from the building, if the building is done.

Q. Did you examine any one part of the building more than another.

A. Yes, sir. I examined the western portion more particularly. It is there that the superficial defects appear, of which I spoke, but all the walls are well lined and well put up.

Q. You regard it as good work?

A. Yes, sir. As a tax-payer, I am satisfied.

Q. You examined the sand, particularly, did you?

A. Yes, sir. I examined it as many times as I have been here.

EXPARTE TESTIMONY.

STATE OF ILLINOIS, }
County of Will. }

Mr. Alexander Gross, being duly sworn, deposeth and says: That he is at present superintendent of the stone department of the Illinois State Penitentiary, which position he has occupied for the past twelve years; that he is a practical stone cutter, and is familiar with both the quantity and quality of all the stone quarried for several past years in the country known as the Desplaines Valley, and considers himself fully competent to judge of the merit and adaptability of stone from the several quarries for the various classes of work. He further states that the stone recently quarried by Mr. Edwin Walker at Lemont is more uniform in color and fully equal in quality to the stone quarried by Messrs. Sanger & Steele, and that there is a difference of from twelve to fifteen per cent. in the cost of sawing and cutting in favor of the stone of Walker's over that of Sanger & Steele's, as tested by him during the past season. ALEXANDER GROSS.

Subscribed and sworn to before me, Henry D. Oakley, Notary Public for the town of Joliet, Will county, Illinois, this - day of February, A. D. 1871.

HENRY D. OAKLEY, Notary Public.

PHILADELPHIA, *May 19th*, 1871.

JOHN MCARTHUR, JR, *Architect, Office 205 South Sixth Strreet:*

DEAR SIR—Yours of the 8th inst. has been received, and would have been answered before, but unavoidable circumstances prevented me.

In answer to your inquiry concerning Mr. Bolin-Starck, as to his claims of being an architect and superintendent of work, and as to his capacity for measuring work, I can say that I never knew him as an architect. As far as I know, he never made plans and superintended a building in this city. He was known among the profession here as a mere draughtsman, and not a very good one at that. He has worked under me, but merely in making *perspective* drawings. I would not trust him to make drawings to go into the hands of any builder (except tracings). Neither would I trust him to superintend the construction of any work, for I do not believe him capable of so doing. I would not trust him to measure or estimate any work for mechanics or otherwise, for I believe he has not the knowledge, capacity or experience so to do. His moral career in this city is not that an honest man might be proud of.

Very truly yours,

W. S. ANDREWS, *Architect.*

---

532 WALNUT STREET, }
Philadelphia, May 11, 1871. }

A. H. PIQUENARD, ESQ., *of Cochrane & Piquenard, Architects Illinois State House:*

MY DEAR SIR:—While it would be a much more pleasant task to me to speak well of one who has been in my service, truth compels me to corroborate your suspicions with reference to C. Bolin-Stark. I have known him since 1858, and have occasionally employed him as draughtsman and colorist, and know that beyond a certain amount of ability as draughtsman, he is utterly without the qualifications of an architect; and *beyond that* he is utterly unworthy of confidence as a man. This may seem a strong expression, but if it fails in any respect, it comes short of the whole truth.

I would not write so, but for the reason that I should thank any friend for telling the truth unreservedly in a similar case.

Very truly yours,
ADDISON HUTTON.

JOHN McARTHUR, JR., *Architect,*
Office 205 *South Sixth Street, Philadelphia, May* 12, 1871.

A. H. PIQUENARD, ESQ., *Architect, Springfield, Ill.:*

DEAR SIR:—Yours of May 8th reached me this morning in my room, where I have been confined with the inflammation of my eyes for the past week. My answer must necessarily be very brief.

Mr. C. Bolin-Stark is well known to the older architects of this city, and while engaged in my office his character, both moral and professional, was not such as to fit him for the responsible position you state he now holds. Not having heard of him for several years, it is possible that he may have chosen a strange city in which to start a new and better life. Should this be the case, I would greatly regret that any testimony of mine should bar his advancement or throw any obstacle in the way of his entire reformation. I think my friend, Mr. Samuel Sloan, architect of this city, can give you much fuller information regarding him, than myself.

Very respectfully,
JOHN McARTHUR, JR.

Per JESSE L. FERGUSON.

OFFICE OF SAMUEL SLOAN, *Architect,*
152 *South Fourth Street, Philadelphia, May* 11*th*, 1871.

A. H. PIQUENARD, *Architect:*

DEAR SIR:—Your favor of the 8th, received, and in answer to your inquries respecting C. Bolin-Stark, I regret that I have not one word to say in his favor, either for his character or his capability to measure, value, or pass judgment upon work. He is not competent to give an opinion on the construction or details of a building.

He never superintended any work in Philadelphia.

I do not believe he was ever in St. Petersburg. I think he would have mentioned the fact to me. *It is a new dodge.* He is a Finn; one of the people whom the Russians hate, and was a hanger-on at my office for many years, from ten to twelve; was brought there by Mr. Harrison, who had contracts in Russia. Stark searched him out upon reaching this country; he could not then speak a word of English, and out of charity I employed him for coloring drawings. He represented himself as a theatrical scene painter. During all the time he did not advance further than coloring. He attempted several perspectives, but never succeeded in bringing the details, from the fact that he had never made architecture a study.

His word is not to be relied upon, and none would trust him, who knew him. He was always in my debt, and is now, for several hundred dollars, besides many others about the city, that have come to my knowledge since his departure.

I have now a warrant for his arrest for false pretense; intended at one time to send an officer for him, but for the great distance and expense, in addition to the risk of its not being recognized by your Governor, and partly upon the promise that he would refund the money, I abandoned it.

The money has never been returned, with the exception of paying the expenses.

I only regret that I cannot do him a favor, but feel it a duty to state the truth, respecting my connection with him.

Respectfully yours,

SAMUEL SLOAN.

MAY 27, 1871.

A. H. PIQUENARD, ESQ.:

DEAR SIR:—I regret the delay in replying to your letter, which happened in consequence of my change of residence, and in answer to your questions, can furnish you with some particulars of Mr. C. B. Stark, who lived some months in my house. He left this city in a very disreputable manner, owing Mr. Sam Sloan about one thousand (1,000) dollars, obtained by false representation, and having obtained furniture to the amount of about three hundred (300) dollars from Mr. Walton, in Walnut street, above Fourth (4th) on false pretenses. For this offense a writ was issued for himself and his wife, concerned also in the conspiracy. And she was arrested and detained in custody some day here, her husband having left her to follow him to Illinois. Finally Mr. Starck arranged and promised to pay a monthly sum towards liquidating his debts, which he has failed to do. The warrant is still out against him, and he will find, some day, a person from here to bring him back to receive his just deserts. He owes me nearly two hundred (200) dollars, which I loaned him under his false representations, and left the city in debt in many other places.

The proceedings against him were instituted in the fall of 1869. With reference to his professional capacity, I do not pretend to judge, but his character as a man is of the very worst. He has proved himself a daring swindler, cheat and liar.

Yours respectfully,

JESSE BARKER, M. D.,

No. 826 Vine street, Philadelphia, Pennsylvania.

EXECUTIVE CHAMBER,
Harrisburg, Pennsylvania, May 27th, 1871.

Messrs. COCHRAN & PIQUENARD, *Architects of Illinois State House:*

GENTLEMEN:—Your letter of the 24th inst., requesting information concerning the moral and professional character of Messrs. McArthur, Sloan, Hutton and Andrews, architects, is received. I am happy to say, in reply, that all of the gentlemen named bear the reputation of being men of the strictest integrity of character, and high standing in their profession, both in Philadelphia and throughout this State.

Yours very truly,

JOHN W. GEARY.

SPRINGFIELD, Feb. 9th, 1869.

To the Board of State House Commissioners for the State of Illinois:

GENTLEMEN:—At your request, we, the undersigned, have visited the location of your proposed State Capitol, and have examined the character and quality of work and material as furnished, and thus far finished, and have also carefully read the requirements of the specifications for the foundation.

In our opinion, the architects have been over cautious in preparing the specifications for said foundations; so much so, that it is hardly practicable to execute them to the letter of the specifications, but substantially the foundations have been put in so as to cover the requirements of the contract, and we have no hesitation in giving it as our opinion, that the foundations are of a very superior character, substantially and scientifically constructed, and capable of supporting a much larger superstructure than you propose to erect upon it, with perfect safety.

As to the quality of stone used in the foundation, we are of the opinion, that while we would not recommend its use for a superstructure, we have no doubt from our own experience, as well as from the reports of Gen. J. H. Wilson, U. S. A., and A. H. Worthen, State Geologist, (both of whom have made more thorough tests and comparisons of this material,) that you have made the best selection of stone you could have done for such a structure.

We have also carefully examined the plans, elevations and sections for your proposed State House; also, the estimate made, and the proposals of responsible parties for the various mechanical works for constructing and finishing the building according to the plans, (most of the individuals furnishing these proposals being personally known to Mr. Boyington, one of the undersigned, who vouches for their reliability,) and have also compared the total of these estimates and proposals with other government and state buildings, (correct data of the cost of which we have as our guide, in addition to the definite proposals made to your architect, by the parties above referred to,) and we find that you can execute the design of your architects in a scientific and substantial manner, for the sum of three millions of dollars ($3,000,000,) and that with the same degree of caution already manifested by your architects, you will have a substantial structure.

Yours respectfully,

WM. M. BOYINGTON, *Architect, Chicago.*
GEO. J. BARNETT, *Architect, St. Louis.*

Senator Fuller, Chairman of sub-committee, then read the report of the nsb-committee, as follows:

To Hon. JOHN COOK, *Chairman of Joint Committee on State House:*

The undersigned, sub-committee, to whom was referred the plans, specifications and estimates for the New State House, submitted by the State House Commissioners, with instruction to employ two disinterested architects and one master-builder, to examine and revise the same, and submit their opinion with reference thereto, beg leave to submit the following report, to-wit:

On the 29th of April, 1869, we met in the city of Chicago, and unanimously agreed upon the appointment of Augustus Bauer and Asher Carter, architects, and Wm. C. Deakman, master-builder, to perform the service aforesaid, and who, after carefully examaning said plans and specifications, and estimating upon the same on the 29th of July last, submitted to us their report in words and figures following:

CHICAGO, July 29, 1869.

Hons. A. C. FULLER, WM. SHEPHERD, A. B. COOK, GEO. W. PARKER, FRANCIS MUNSON, *Committee:*

GENTLEMEN:—The undersigned having been, on the 29th of April, appointed to examine the plans and specifications, and make estimates of the proposed New State House, and having been instructed by you to carefully revise and verify the same, and report to you our opinion of the merits and correctness of the same, and also to suggest any changes or modifications of the same, which in our opinion ought to be made, would respectfully report—

That soon after our appointment we entered upon the discharge of our duties, and having carefully and fully considered the whole matter submitted to us, we have visited Springfield and examined the foundation now nearly completed, at an expense, we are advised, of about $450,000, for a New State House, and without expressing any opinion as to whether said foundation is according to the specifications, we are of the opinion that the foundation is substantial, and that the superstructure contemplated by the plan may be safely placed upon it, provided such portions of said foundation as are now covered are constructed in the same manner as the work exposed. We cannot express an opinion as to the abstract merits of the general plan of the superstructure as compared with others. We are satisfied that the general plan may be adopted, and, with several important changes and modifications, which are hereinafter mentioned, the whole building, when completed, will be a tasteful, convenient and permanent structure, worthy of the people of the state. The estimates of the cost of the various parts of the work, submitted by you, contain, in our opinion, more or less important differences in estimates.

The estimated cost of the cut stone work, as submitted, was $1,032,943. Our estimate for the same is $1,114,646 65. The estimate for marble work is $241,516; our estimate for the same is $121,726 19. The estimate for the brick and concrete is $273,584; our estimate for the same is $390,761 13, besides $8,000 for building centres for arches—making a total of $398,761 13. The estimate for plastering and ornamental work is $62,177; our estimate for the same is $81,868 80. The estimate for carpenter and joiner work is $185,000; our estimate for the same is $212,212 95. The estimate for roofing, gutters flushing etc., is $45,714; our estimate for the same is $51,000 66.

The estimate for cast and wrought iron work is $600,000; our estimate for cast iron work is $248,928 16, and for wrought iron work, is $208,039 30, making a total of $540,965 46. To this should be added iron stairway leading from the gallery floor to dome lantern, which is not specified nor only partly shown on plans, costing $10,883 58. The estimate for zinc ornaments is $2,500; our estimate for the same is $3,049 20. The estimate for gas fitting and plumbing is $23,000; our estimate for the same is $14,505, which includes also cost of marble partition in place of wood (as per specifications) between urinals. The estimate for painting, glazing and frescoing is $86,951; our estimate for the same is $83,321 24. The estimate for heating and ventilating is $97,500; our estimate for the same is $105,000.

It will be seen from the foregoing, that the total estimate above named is $2,650,885, and that our estimate for the same, based upon the plans and specifications submitted, is $2,737,940 86.

Having specially and carefully examined the plans with reference to the practicability and fitness of the proposed building for the purposes intended, we would urgently recommend the following changes and modifications:

1st. The plan provides for wood partitions for second and third stories; also for wood roof and galleries; also for plastered wood ceiling throughout the building. It is evident that the buiding, thus constructed with the above mentioned materials, would be dangerous, on account of liability to destruction by fire; and, in this connection, it may be added that experience in the construction of such buildings has shown to be necessary what the law authorizing the erection of a new state house requires, that it shall be as near fire proof as possible.

We, therefore, in consideration of safety and durability, recommend that the above mentioned portions of said building be constructed of iron and zinc instead of wood. We have, therefore, made an appropriate estimate of the additional cost of these changes, and find it to be about $150,000.

2d. We also recommend that the floors of the rotunda and the halls of the basement be of marble instead of Joliet flagging; also, the hall floors of the second and third stories to be of marble, instead of wood; also, that the columns, pilasters, arches, rails and balusters inclosing the grand stairway be marble instead of iron; also, the wainscoting and soffits of grand stairway be of marble instead of plaster, because such change is necessary to make the whole work harmonize. The plans now show iron in connection with marble, which is objectionable in an architecural point of view. The additional cost of the last mentioned changes would be about $110,000.

3d. We also recommend iron stairs in west wing, leading from second to third stories, to be of iron instead of wood. The additional cost of this will be about $4,500.

4th. We further recommend that the rotunda floor lights be of prismatic lights, instead of hammered glass, adding to cost about $3,600.

5th. We further recommend that all outside windows and inside doors be glazed with polished plate glass, instead of double French glass. The additional cost of this will be about $25,000.

6th. We further recommend that fire places be provided for all the principal rooms of the first story and basement. This will require the erection of cut stone chimney tops, increasing the cost of cut stone according to the number and design of chimneys erected. No considerable additional cost for mantle pieces and grates is required, as they can be put in at any future time in the prepared mason work. It will be seen that the total additional cost of the above specified changes and modifications recommended by us as important, is $293,100, and which, added to the amount of our estimates based on the plans and specifications submitted, amount to $3,031,040 86, as the entire cost of the building above the foundation.

We are informed that the late law concerning the New State House limits the cost of the building, exclusive of such foundation, to $3,000,000. We are of the opinion that at the present prices for material and work more than the above excess of $31,000 may be saved by modifications in omitting certain portions of the work without impairing the general appearance or intrinsic value of the building. There are other minor but important changes which we think should be made, but which we do not regard necessary to here specify, and which doubtless will suggest themselves to the supervising architect during the progress of the work. In view of the fact that the proposed edifice is intended to be permanent, and the great expense attending its construction, we would, in conclusion, suggest the propriety and importance of using great care in selecting the materials to be used in its construction.

Accompanying this report are submitted our detailed estimates, and which are marked exhibit "A."

[Signed]

AUGUSTUS BAUER, *Architect.*
ASHER CARTER, *Architect.*
W. C. DEAKMAN, *Builder.*

The foregoing report, in our opinion, contains several important recommendations by said architects and master builder, but as the undersigned are unable to unanimously agree upon any recommendation to your committee concerning the adoption of the original plans for said State House, we beg leave to submit said report, and the plans, specifications and estimates therein referred to, for the consideration of the general committee, without the expression, on our part, of an opinion concerning the merits of the same.

We also submit the bill of said architects and builder for services rendered, also the bill for printing said specifications, as directed by the general committee. All of which is respectfully submitted.

Dated at Springfield, August 26, 1869.

[Signed]

ALLEN C. FULLER,
WM. SHEPHERD,
ANSEL B. COOK,
FRANCIS MUNSON,
GEO. W. PARKER.

Mr. Cook, of Lake, then, at the request of the committee, explained the propriety of the changes suggested by the revising architects, as stated at length in the report.

Mr. Parker moved the adoption of the following resolution, the motion being seconded by Mr. Coy:

WHEREAS, It appears to the satisfaction of this committee, that the New State House, constructed in accordance with the plans and specifications submitted by the State House Commissioners, with the necessary changes recommended by the revising architects and master builder, can be completed for $3,000,000, exclusive of the amount already expended on the foundation; and that the building, when completed, will be a beautiful, convenient and permanent structure, worthy of the State; therefore,

Resolved, That the plans and specifications for a New State House, submitted by the State Commissioners, including the changes proposed by the revising architects and master builder in their report to the sub-committee, so far as the same may tend to render the building, when completed, safe, harmonious, and as near fire-proof as possible, be, and the same are hereby approved; and the said State House Commissioners are hereby authorized to proceed in the construction of said State House in accordance with the same.

The resolution was adopted by the following vote:

Yeas—Messrs. Fort, Strevell, Nicholson, Cook, of Sangamon, Coy, Parker, Cook of Lake, Palmer, Bradshaw, Dinsmoor, Munson, Morgan, and Fuller of Jersey—13.

Nays—Messrs. Ward, Fuller of Boone, Crawford and Shepherd—4.

[COPY.]

MAYOR'S OFFICE, CHICAGO, MAY 24, 1871.

JOHN F. BARNARD, Esq.:

Dear Sir—I have carefully examined the mason work of the new State House at Springfield, Illinois, and do not see how there could be any great difference of opinion among those competent to judge. In several places quite large holes had been opened through the walls, giving me a good opportunity to see the interior work; and I feel no hesitation in saying, that the material is uniformly good and the work uniformly well done. In some cases mortar, used in the brick work, is of quick lime and some cases of water lime. I should give the preference to water lime, although both are good of their kind. The walls are well in line, throughout, and have apparently been laid with great care; and I did not discover any defect, in the material or workmanship, that would, in any way, affect the stability of the building. I am quite sure if there be any failure in the work thus far, it will not be on account of bad material or bad workmanship.

Very respectfully yours,

R. B. MASON.

www.ingramcontent.com/pod-product-compliance
Lightning Source LLC
LaVergne TN
LVHW011217110826
845150LV00006B/1454

* 9 7 8 1 4 2 5 5 1 6 7 1 0 *